THE COMPLETE
MINI

THE COMPLETE
MINI

CHRIS REES

MRP

MOTOR RACING PUBLICATIONS LTD
Unit 6, The Pilton Estate, 46 Pitlake, Croydon CR0 3RY, England

First published 1994

British Library Cataloguing in Publication Data

Rees, Chris
  Complete Mini
  I. Title
  629.2222

ISBN 0-947981-88-8

Typesetting and origination by Ryburn Publishing Services,
Keele University Press, Staffordshire
Printed in Great Britain by The Amadeus Press Ltd,
Huddersfield, West Yorkshire

Contents

Acknowledgements

I would like to thank everyone who has kindly offered their help in the course of producing this book, whether in the supply of information and photographs or merely through their advice.

In particular I would like to thank Gary Axon for the use of his Mini brochure collection, John Blunsden and the MRP archive, David Johns of Duncan Hamilton, Ian Strachan and Kevin Jones of Rover Product Affairs, Karam Ram and Rex Trueman of the BMIHT archive, Simon Empson of Broadspeed Engineering, Chris Cheal, Adrian Boyns, Martin Bell, Phillip Splett and, finally, Mark Vellenoweth and Tim Nuttall of the Mini Moke Club.

September 1994   C R

The designation LE stands for Limited Edition, yet there seems to be no limit to the variations on the Mini theme, which have helped to sustain and enhance the enthusiasm for Sir Alec Issigonis' brilliant concept more than a third of a century after the first examples travelled down the BMC production lines at Longbridge and Cowley. To emphasize the Mini's global appeal, this derivative was marketed by the New Zealand Motor Corporation in 1977, its special features including wheel trims, side stripes, a matt black grille, a vinyl roof, a carpeted boot, a leather gear knob and brushed nylon seats and facia. A Clubman version was also sold.

SECTION ONE
Genesis

After 35 years in production, the Mini has become the very thing it bucked against: an institution. The difference is, the Mini is a much-loved and much-respected institution. It was a pioneer in the art of transverse front-wheel drive, a marvel of packaging and a testament to the conquest of technical barriers. A genuine revolution when it was launched in 1959, it became such a familiar sight all round the world that it eventually became an establishment in its own right.

The Mini's story is all the more remarkable in that it was almost entirely the brainchild of one man – Alec Issigonis – and was probably the last mass-produced car ever designed by one person alone. It is unlike any other car seen either before or since, and there can be nothing but admiration for it, for its brilliant designer and for the courageous management which gave the go-ahead to such a revolutionary product.

The birth of the Mini took place in an era when austerity and shortages were still the norm. In the Fifties, European drivers did not have much of a disposable income and petrol was still rationed in many countries. It was an age of 'economy cars', an age when bubble cars like the Heinkel and Isetta were selling in their tens of thousands.

Just as the world economy was pulling itself out of the ashes of the devastation wreaked during the Second World War, the Suez oil crisis hit in September 1956. The Egyptian dictator, Nasser, had cut the oil lifeline to the west by occupying the Suez Canal, and for all anyone knew, there might be an indefinite shortage of oil; meanwhile, British drivers were rationed to 10 gallons of petrol a month.

Against this backdrop, the British Motor Corporation's Chairman, Leonard Lord, realized there was a potentially huge market for a cheap small car which combined economy with large-car characteristics. To whom could he entrust the task of developing such a car?

There was one obvious, but brave choice: Alec Issigonis. Born in Smyrna in 1906, Issigonis had come to Britain to study at the age of 15. When he had finished his education at Battersea Tech, he got a job in a London design office in 1928 working on an automatic clutch, and from there he went on to work briefly for Humber.

However, Issigonis' career did not really take off until he joined Britain's leading car manufacturer, Morris, in 1936. This was where he met Leonard Lord, on a team designing suspensions. Issigonis developed wishbone suspension for Morris before the war, although because of the hostilities it did not make it into production until the MG YA of 1949.

During the war, in between military projects, Issigonis had begun work on a small car for Morris which was soon to become his first complete road car: the Morris Minor. So pressing at that time was the need of the Nuffield Organisation (of which Morris was now a part) for such a small car that the Minor was rushed into production in 1948 without some of Issigonis' planned innovations. Yet it did have several advanced features including integral body/chassis construction, rack-and-pinion steering and torsion-bar front suspension. By 1952, a prototype was also running with front-wheel drive, but this never became a production reality for the Minor – and could certainly not have happened after the Austin/Nuffield merger in 1952, when the Austin 803cc OHV engine replaced the archaic 918cc Morris side-valve engine.

Issigonis left the newly-formed but bureaucracy-bound British Motor Corporation to work for Alvis on a brand-new sports saloon. This was

The father of the Mini: (Sir) Alec Issigonis.

Part of the genius of Alec Issigonis was his ability to sketch out drawings which his team of draughtsmen would then translate into technical illustrations. His sketching talent has been likened to Leonardo da Vinci's.

to have had a new 3.5-litre aluminium V8 and a full-width body designed by Issigonis. Although it was a three-box saloon, some striking design similarities can be traced between the Alvis and Issigonis' later work for BMC. The sports saloon was doomed, however, as Alvis' other investment demands starved the project of cash.

So Issigonis returned to the BMC fold in 1956 when Lord asked him to join the design office to work on a new medium-sized family saloon. Project XC9001 showed the way Issigonis was

now thinking: a two-box full-width saloon body with a drop-down tailgate – the very essentials of the Mini package. However, this was very much larger than the eventual Mini and was designed for rear-wheel drive (XC9001 would eventually develop into the Austin/Morris 1800).

Then the Suez crisis hit and Leonard Lord was quickly convinced of the importance of a BMC economy car. In March 1957, he told Issigonis to drop his work on XC9001 and begin development on the small car project, which assumed the title

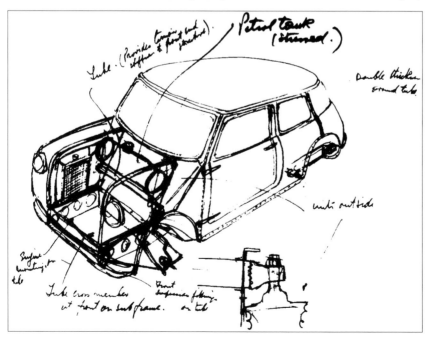

This early rendering shows the familiar basic profile and seam welds, as well as rejected ideas like a front-mounted fuel tank. Note the original position of the radiator on the offside.

ADO15. Assembling a small team around him, Issigonis initiated the genesis of the Mini.

Although, inevitably, various other people were involved in its creation, it was essentially one man's car, which was to be the Mini's great strength and the source of its perennial charm.

Issigonis dictated the car's specifics from day one with the sort of arrogance that today's committee designers would find intolerable. The essential factor for the new small car was that it should be able to carry four adults in comfort, plus their luggage. Issigonis calculated the space needed for the passengers and concluded that a cube 104in long by 50in wide by 52in tall would be needed. That dictated the cabin shape and size.

Issigonis became obsessed with the need to save space. With the Minor, he had already attempted, unsuccessfully, to introduce the greatest space-saving principle of all: front-wheel drive. All the space needed for the propshaft and final drive could be knocked out by incorporating it all at the front, and from the start he knew that he would have to use front-wheel drive for the Mini.

The big question was what engine to use. Lord insisted that Issigonis make use of an existing BMC engine on grounds of cost, so the only obvious choice was the A-series unit as found in the Austin A35 and Morris Minor. The trouble was, this powertrain measured 38in from stem to stern, and this, in Issigonis' view, would eat up too much space. There was some experiment with a two-cylinder engine (basically an A-series engine chopped in half), but although this made the engine shorter, it was an impossibly rough-running unit.

Then Issigonis had a leap of the imagination. What if the gearbox could be placed under the crankshaft, instead of behind? The engine and gearbox would effectively become one unit and could be mounted transversely, driving each front wheel.

Transverse engines were by no means new, having been seen even before the war and were currently in use in, for instance, the Lloyd micro-car. However, the gearbox being slung under the engine certainly was new. The lubrication problem was simply overcome by plumbing the gearbox into the engine so that it could use the same sump oil supply.

By putting the engine and gearbox together across the engine bay – and so being able to remove the radiator from its normal front position to the side – the length of the A-series powertrain dropped by a proportionally enormous margin.

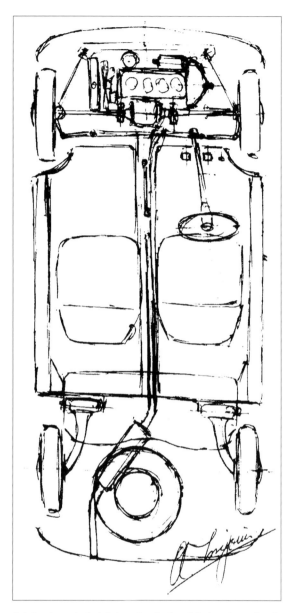

A later layout sketch bearing Issigonis' signature clearly shows the impact larger wheels would have had on rear passenger space. By now, the radiator is on the nearside.

It was felt that the A35's 803cc engine would not provide the performance and smoothness which the new car would require, so the decision was taken to expand the A-series engine to 948cc by boring it out to 62.94mm. Yet on tests, the engine – which was quite capable of developing very high outputs – gave the little car *too much* performance – it was tested to beyond 90mph, with only 37bhp on tap.

So it was taken back down to 848cc by reducing

XC 9003 was the first full-size representation of Issigonis' ideas for the BMC economy car. Running prototypes (called 'Orange Boxes') were built using this 1957 Austin mock-up as their cue.

the stroke from 73.72mm to 68.26mm. At this stage, it was running with the radiator on the offside and the inlet valves and carburettor to the front. When it was found that the large primary gears between the clutch and geartrain were too much for the synchromesh to handle, the engine was turned round 180 degrees so that smaller gearwheels could be used. The radiator ended up on the nearside.

When combined with widening the Mini bodyshell by 2 inches at around the same time – which increased air resistance considerably – the top speed of the Mini dropped from 92mph to a more manageable 74mph. This was still unusually good by the standards of the late Fifties.

In order to provide drive to the wheels without affecting the way the Mini steered, Issigonis had to make use of newly-developed universal joints. The power was transmitted through ball bearings in the joint, which effectively eliminated the tendency for the driveshafts to try to straighten out under power while cornering. Another major hurdle in the refinement of a workable front-

wheel drive system had been cleared.

Issigonis was always strongly in favour of small wheels: the 14in wheels of the 1948 Morris Minor were easily the smallest of any saloon of its day, but the Mini went much further: its 10in diameter wheels were far and away the smallest used in any car, except for some true microcars which used scooter wheels. The sole reason for such small wheels was a sacrifice to the great god of packaging: they freed up more interior space by reducing the intrusion of the inner wheelarches.

The main disadvantage of 10in wheels was the harsh ride they were expected to give over rough surfaces. Yet here again Issigonis was ahead of the objectors. From his days with Morris, when he had joined forces with Alex Moulton to build a rubber-sprung Morris Minor, and later with Alvis, Issigonis had become a convert to the idea of rubber suspension. He knew that Moulton was still working on rubber suspension systems, and such an arrangement, said Issigonis' intuition, would provide the necessary pliancy with an ability to stiffen-up under load. It did: the rubber

The Mini was used as the basis for other in-house projects. The car on the left is a 1958 styling study for an 'enlarged Mini', which would soon evolve into the Morris 1100. To give an idea of its size, it is shown alongside one of Issigonis' other brilliant inventions: the Morris Minor.

George Harriman (left) with Issigonis and one of the first production cars. Harriman had become Managing Director of BMC in 1958 and was as enthusiastic as Leonard Lord about the Mini. It was he who gave the go-ahead for the Mini-Cooper.

cone system was so effective that it is still used on the Mini today. The independent front suspension followed Morris Minor practice, with forged links and a tie-rod, while at the rear there were trailing arms mounted in needle bearings.

The first two prototypes ran with their engines attached directly to the bodywork. After extensive testing, the metal around the mounting points was found to be suffering from severe fatigue. This brought about the Mini's construction around subframes. All the major components – engine, gearbox, suspension, steering – were mounted into one subframe at the front, with a further subframe at the back to carry the rear suspension. This also eliminated a lot of vibration and would prove invaluable in the development of a wide range of Mini derivatives which could use these subframe assemblies completely unaltered.

Weight distribution was initially too light at the back, leading to the rear wheels locking up under hard braking, hence it was decided to move the battery from under the bonnet to the boot. A Lockheed pressure-limiting valve was also fitted for the rear brakes.

Keeping costs to an absolute minimum meant accommodating such measures as exposed seams in the bodywork to allow easy spot-welding of the main body sections, exposed door hinges simply bolted to the main hull and a lack of winding windows or elaborate door handle mechanisms.

By November 1957, the first prototypes were running. In July 1958, Leonard Lord drove one of the 'Orange Boxes' – so called because of their paint scheme – and was so impressed with it that he simply told Issigonis to have it in production as it stood within 12 months.

This interesting sectional view of the 1959 Mini perfectly displays the miracle of packaging it represented. The drivetrain occupies a tiny space, while the cabin boasts an extremely high proportional volume of the car as a whole. Note the direct gear linkage.

11

Project 9X was the car that might have replaced the Mini. Designed by Issigonis and constructed by a team headed by John Sheppard in 1968, it would have been the world's first three-door hatchback. Two BMC design chiefs discuss its finer points: the bespectacled Dick Burzi and 'Ben' Benbow.

Unsurprisingly, perhaps, given the incredibly short development period of the prototypes, the Mini entered production with many faults still requiring resolution. The most notorious of these was water intrusion, caused by lapping the sills the wrong way. After an exceptionally dry summer in 1959, the problem had not come to light, but during the torrential downpours of the following winter, it did not take customers long to notice their door bins and footwells filling up with water.

The first Minis of all were built on April 4, 1959 at BMC's Longbridge plant, when three pre-production cars were put together virtually by hand. The first Morris Mini-Minor (the car later registered 621 AOK) was built at Cowley on May 8, and still survives today in the hands of the British Motor Industry Heritage Trust.

By August 1959, the most important car in BMC's history was ready to be launched. Alec Issigonis had done it – and done it in less than two-and-a-half years. Ironically, given its huge success, the Mini was the last car designed completely by Issigonis. The subsequent BMC 1100 and 1800 models were logical progressions of the Mini theme, but Issigonis preferred experiment to fitting in with corporate design committees, and it was left to others to see his concepts through to production. He was knighted in 1969 and retired in 1971, although he remained a consultant to BL. Active until the end, he died, aged 81, in October 1988.

Issigonis was always scathing of both marketing men and 'stylists'. He was utterly anti-styling, believing that its effect was simply to add weight to cars. He thought of himself not as a designer, but as an 'ironmonger'. The Mini evolved entirely from logical precepts with not even the remotest accession to style. It was the perfect expression of his ideals of engineering out excess weight and extracting the most from the least.

The Mini was the embodiment of Issigonis' engineering genius, and of all his personal foibles. He said: "Small cars all look the same because they are designed by committees trying to copy the Mini." With typical arrogance, he believed that what he thought was good practice was good for everyone else. In the Mini's case, he may actually have been right.

On his retirement from BL in 1971, Sir Alec Issigonis standing proudly beside his most celebrated baby; 621 AOK was the very first Mini to be produced (on May 8, 1959). A basic Morris Mini-Minor, it still runs on the roads today and can usually be seen at the British Motor Industry Heritage Trust Museum at Gaydon.

Austin and Morris Minis (1959–69)

The date was August 18, 1959; the place, the British Army testing ground at Chobham, Surrey. The world's press had gathered by invitation to witness and drive the British Motor Corporation's brand-new small cars for the very first time.

These were the long-awaited Morris Mini-Minor and Austin Se7en: the much-rumoured revolutionary replacement for the Austin A35 had arrived at last. It was not entirely a surprise, as scoop photographs had appeared as early as spring 1959 in the French magazine *L'Auto-Journal*, and prototypes had become a familiar sight in the Oxfordshire countryside since 1958.

Yet nothing could have prepared the assembled journalists for the motoring revelation they were about to experience. The little car looked completely unique, behaved in a different class from any other economy car and swallowed more people and luggage than was decent for even a much larger saloon.

BMC's brave new car received its official public launch on the international stage on August 26, 1959 in a blaze of publicity. National adverts proclaimed: "You've never seen a car like this before", stating it to be "the most revolutionary small car ever built". For once, one could admit that the advertising copy was not all hype.

Morris' adverts proclaimed: "It's Wizardry on Wheels", while one of the colourful Austin ads piped: "Just try to find the ordinary in an Austin Seven". And it was true: the new Mini was as different from the British small car norm in 1959 as a space shuttle from a firework. It bristled with innovative ideas, it looked radically different from any other car and was the most compact 'real' car Britain had ever produced.

the incredible new AUSTIN se7en

The revolutionary design of the Austin Se7en was highlighted in early publicity. This 1959 illustration spotlights the features which would have been unfamiliar to car buyers, like the engine lubrication system, rubber suspension and front-wheel drive. Buyers were initially suspicious of so much innovation.

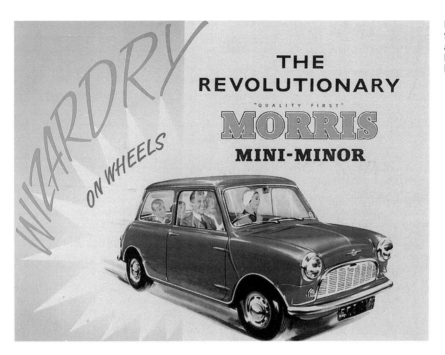

The Mini's engine was a direct development of the 803cc A-series engine first used in the 1951 Austin A30. In its final production form, expanded to 848cc, it was fitted with a single SU carburettor (made by BMC) and developed 34bhp. BMC claimed a top speed of 74mph and 0–60mph acceleration in 17 seconds. Magazine tests confirmed the top speed, but the test cars were never able to match the acceleration figures: a typical 0–60mph time was the 26.5sec recorded by *The Autocar*. This was quite adequate for the Mini at a time when most of the competition – which in 1960 BMC identified principally as the Fiat 600D, Renault Dauphine, Ford Anglia 105E, VW Beetle and Triumph Herald – were notable for their sluggish performance; only the Anglia was faster, at 76mph and 0–60mph in 16.5sec.

However, none of the Mini's rivals could remotely match its handling. On launch, BMC described it as having 'dart-like' stability and the front-wheel-drive layout was claimed to "take you round corners like a sportscar". Again, that was no idle claim. As almost every major manufacturer subsequently discovered, front-wheel drive in a small car provides sharp, predictable and safe roadholding. The Mini was a natural understeerer, like all front-drive cars, and in no small measure, but that was a quantum leap forward compared with the tail-happy behaviour of the competition – especially the rear-engined continental cars.

The front suspension broadly followed the layout of Issigonis' Morris Minor: single links above and below the driveshafts, located by a tie-rod with rubber mountings. At the rear, each wheel, along with the hub and brake drum, was suspended by a trailing arm mounted on a needle bearing. The Mini was very nearly the first British small car with all-round independent suspension (the Triumph Herald beat it by a matter of months).

Where the suspension departed from BMC practice – and everyone else's – was in its use of rubber cones in place of springs. Each suspension unit – one for each corner – comprised an inner and outer cone with rubber bonded in between, mounted in a strut. In use, the cones compressed as the car encountered obstacles, and gave a consistent response to bumps in the road.

The ride engendered by this set-up was adjudged to be excellent for the time, although there was some harshness on rough roads, partly due to the unusually small diameter of the wheels. Indeed, no mass-production car capable of the Mini's speeds had ever been made, so special 10in tyres had to be developed by Dunlop.

Rubber-cone suspension was abandoned on standard Minis from 1964–69 in favour of Hydrolastic, but was then reinstated for the MkII Mini. From then on, the Mini never looked back, a fact which endorses the effectiveness of the dry system. However, as the years rolled on, the

The incredibly compact drivetrain is well illustrated by this Austin cutaway display car.

Mini's ride inevitably became increasingly criticized for its joggliness.

Combined with their nimble performance and diminutive size, Minis were perfect for town and city driving, able to perform manoeuvres previously reserved for light sportscars and motorbikes.

They were also pretty good in competition, as the Mini-Cooper would soon show. Even before the arrival of the all-conquering Coopers, standard Minis were scoring significant wins in saloon car racing and autotests, although as a rule the Mini was not favoured as a competition car. This was partly due to BMC's policy of offering works

cars only in standard tune. However, there were successes: Pat Moss achieved an early win in a minor event in 1959 and there was a class win in the 1960 Geneva Rally with Don and Erle Morley at the controls, while in May 1960, John Handley's Mini finished 10th overall in the Dutch Tulip Rally. By 1961, there was enough interest in Minis for the British Racing and Sports Car Club to launch a one-make race for Minis.

However, competition use did have one side-effect: it quickly exposed some failings of the early design. The oil seal problem (see below) put many cars out of action, while hard cornering revealed a problem with the wheels: they were just not strong enough and often simply shattered. BMC was forced to make new, stronger steel wheels for all Minis from 1961.

Although the smaller-engined Minis were eclipsed by the Mini-Cooper from 1961 onward, they remained a popular and affordable way to race. Sir John Whitmore's 848cc Mini won the British Saloon Car Championship in 1961. By 1964, however, the club racers' 850cc saloon car class had all but vanished, leading the 750 Motor Club to form its own Mini Se7en Formula in 1967 for under-850cc entrants, rejuvenating interest in Mini racing.

Yet performance and agility were not the main objectives in the design of the Mini: they were simply the result of the engineering brilliance of the design. Economy of use was cited by BMC as a more important element in the Mini formula at the time of its launch. Indeed, the Mini was intended first and foremost to be affordable

Production gets underway at Longbridge in 1959. The assembly line at Austin's well-equipped factory shared space with the A40 production line.

15

Much of the launch publicity stressed the new car's carrying capacity. All this luggage would apparently fit in, no doubt stuffed into the door bins, under the seats and on top of the fold-down bootlid.

transport for the masses. The original advertising boasted of 'penny-a-mile' running costs, based on the claim that the car could do 50mpg at a constant 50mph. Thanks to its light overall weight, it returned mileages far superior to those of its main competitors. Probably only the Fiat 500 and 600 were more economical.

Packaging was the Mini's trump card. Priority was given to creating and making use of as much interior space as possible. The front-drive layout eliminated the need for a transmission tunnel and what would now be called the Mini's 'two-box' design created almost the maximum possible interior volume. The amount of legroom available for all passengers was striking. It was indeed superior to all the Mini's rivals, including much larger cars like the VW Beetle and Ford Anglia.

Another neat packaging idea was designing a bootlid which folded down, allowing it to double-up as an occasional luggage platform, which was fairly useful because the boot was tiny, having to share its space with the fuel tank and battery. The

rear number-plate was hinged along its top so that it could still be seen when loaded up – a fitment which lasted right up until the Clubman. BMC even designed wicker baskets to go under the rear seats in an effort to use every available square foot of space, but these never actually went into production. Instead, BMC suggested you slide your own picnic hamper into the space under the seats.

Inside, there were deep door pockets for all four passengers. Wind-down windows could not be incorporated, so the front passengers had sliding ones instead and the rear passengers in the De Luxe models could hinge their windows outwards.

If the interior was a miracle of packaging, it was also a very sparse place to be – a deliberate move on behalf of Issigonis and the BMC product-planners. There were basic and De Luxe versions, but even the latter had thin seat squabs and plenty of bare painted metal and just one solitary round instrument dial. This incorporated a speedometer, fuel gauge and warning lights for oil

One of the first Austin Se7ens built. This is a De Luxe model.

An absolutely basic Se7en was a rarity, but this was the entry level for customers. There was no bright trim around the arches, sills or screens, the wheels came without embellishers, the rear quarter-windows were fixed and there were no screen washers. *(BMIHT)*

pressure, dynamo charge and high-beam headlights. There was a lamp set into the side of the instrument nacelle with a little switch to operate it. The pushbutton starter was located on the floor, shrouded to prevent accidental operation.

The cabin reflected many of Issigonis' own prejudices. It lacked any provision for a radio, for instance, because he disapproved of them (when they were fitted, they always had a tacked-on appearance). Another Issigonis foible prevented the car being designed with seat belts in mind and, indeed, these remained an option for many years. It also meant that, if the driver wore his seat belt, he could not reach the gear-lever or dash-mounted switches. These problems were not addressed until the Mini MkII, when long toggle switches and a remote gearchange were introduced.

The biggest single change to the basic Mini's specification had to be the Hydrolastic suspension system fitted from September 1964. Issigonis had always wanted this feature on the Mini, but was denied on the grounds of cost. Finally he got his way. As fitted to the Mini, it was described by BMC as "the greatest suspension ever!"

The Hydrolastic system had been under development by Issigonis and Alex Moulton for seven years. It had first made its appearance on the Morris 1100 in August 1962, and had proven its effectiveness in practice. The reason why Hydrolastic was developed for the Mini – at quite some expense – was that the dry rubber cone system had a rather choppy ride which varied according to temperature. Hydrolastic was intended to eliminate pitch and provide a superior ride.

The De Luxe version of the Austin Se7en could be recognized externally by its standard chrome wheeltrims, bright plastic inserts for the front and rear screens, vivid plastic sill and wheelarch finishers, hinging rear quarter-lights with bright frames, chrome fuel filler cap, chrome number-plate surround and twin-jet washers.

The basic model's interior really was basic. The floor covering was thin, loose and made of rubber and most of the interior was bare painted metal. The only difference between Austin and Morris interiors was the steering boss badge (this a Morris version). Note the floor-mounted starter button and absence of a heater. *(BMIHT)*

Hydrolastic worked via a water/anti-freeze/corrosion-inhibitor fluid system. This was sealed for life into maintenance-free cylinders, which fitted neatly into the subframes. Springing was still by rubber, but each front suspension unit was interconnected via pipework to its corresponding unit at the rear.

Each unit consisted of a cylinder with a lower rubber diaphragm, a damper valve and an upper rubber doughnut which was rather like the original dry cone of the early Mini. When a front wheel hit a bump, most of the impact was absorbed by the fluid being forced up into the cylinder, the top rubber doughnut acting as a spring. Some of the fluid was displaced through a hole in the rubber doughnut, flowing back along the pipework and entering the rear Hydrolastic unit, which raised the rear suspension by a small amount – a basic self-levelling effect. When two wheels on the same side simultaneously encountered a bump, the fluid in the whole side's system became pressurized and the effective springing reverted to the rubber cones.

Yet there were problems. The system still reacted to outside temperature and there was initially a tendency for the units to squeak (remedied by modifying the damper valves). The

biggest problem was that, when fully loaded, the rear end sagged badly, causing the headlamps to illuminate the heavens. The German authorities banned Hydrolastic for this reason, so Minis for the German market always retained the old dry suspension. Far from relieving the pitch effect, when accelerating or braking hard, the Hydrolastic system caused the front end to rise and fall by about 3 inches. The overall improvement to the ride was only slight and, while its reliability record was good, there was a tendency for the system to lose pressure over time and produce the 'sagging Mini' effect.

These problems came in addition to the extra cost involved in manufacturing the Hydrolastic system, so its life expectancy was always in danger. In fact, it lasted for only five years on the Mini saloon, although it remained on the Mini-Cooper right up until its demise in 1971. It was never fitted to the longer-wheelbase load-carrying estate, van or pick-up. The system was simply too expensive to manufacture for the perceived benefits and the production lines reverted to fitting the old dry-cone suspension once more from the Mini MkII of August 1969.

It has been said many times that the Mini as introduced in 1959 was too cheap. At £497, it was

18

pretty much the cheapest proper car on sale in Britain (only the archaic Ford Popular, at £419, was cheaper). In prewar terms, that equated to less than £100, the price of the very cheapest and starkest British wares. That price actually fell, reaching an all-time low of just £448 between 1962 and 1964, when it even undercut Ford's new Popular 100E. It is most unlikely that in those early days BMC ever made any money on the Mini.

Yet in practice, most people opted for the more expensive De Luxe models, which were only slightly less expensive than the model they replaced: the Austin A35 De Luxe. Many potential customers could not see the attraction of the new car. Its openly revolutionary design was regarded with suspicion by most first-time buyers as too radical. The wealthier middle classes may have admired it, but thought it too minimal for their status-conscious existences. Indeed, it took a long while before people realized what a brilliant package the Mini was and began to accept it.

In the end, it was an unexpected class of buyer which actually gave the Mini its sales momentum. Despite the fact that Issigonis hated the idea of cars being status symbols, the Mini ended up becoming one of the biggest status symbols of them all. Trendy Londoners started to buy the Mini for its city abilities: it was small enough to leap through tiny gaps in traffic, had an excellent turn of speed and needed only an 11ft 6in gap in which to park. Above all, it also had that essential element of 'cool'. Inevitably, it became a cult object and fashion accessory, attracting owners prepared to spend often large sums of money on upgrading the basic machine. In their wake, the Mini finally caught on on a large-scale with the general public. Some good publicity was harvested when Issigonis took Queen Elizabeth II for a spin in a Mini around Windsor Great Park.

The Mini's sluggish start can be appreciated from the sales figures. Only 19,749 cars were made in 1959 and the true vintage years of Mini production did not occur until the early Seventies, when annual production exceeded 300,000. The best-ever year was some 12 years after the Mini's launch, in 1971, when some 318,475 were made. The growing momentum of Mini sales can be judged by the fact that the millionth Mini was not made until six years into its production life in 1965, the two millionth in 1969 and the three millionth in 1972.

The key to BMC's marketing strategy – determined to a large extent by its partisan separate-

Inside the De Luxe, you were treated to kickplates on the door pockets, a passenger's sun visor, chrome surround to the facia switch panel, vinyl fabric covering for the dash, ashtrays and lights in the rear pockets, carpets on the floor and front wheelarches, headlining on the rear quarter-panels, leathercloth-type trim casings below waist level, standard heater and more comfortable seat cushions. *(BMIHT)*

marque dealer network – was a proliferation of badge-engineered models. Both Austin and Morris versions of the Mini saloon and estate car were introduced, both selling at exactly the same price with only badges and front grilles to distinguish them. The multi-faceted Mini range just grew bigger and bigger: by 1961 there were also Mini-Coopers, the booted Riley Elf and Wolseley Hornet, plus Mini estate, van and pick-up variants; and there had been a prototype Mini Moke running since 1959.

The Mini was subject to a host of minor revisions almost from the very start. Since the car had evolved in such a short period, there were inevitably problems caused by lack of development. Indeed, the early Mini quickly gained a reputation for unreliability and BMC suffered a deluge of warranty claims.

One of the chief culprits was the oil seal at the

The early De Luxe dashboard. Note the black-on-white speedometer (changed to white-on-black from 1964) and recirculatory heater under the switch panel.

From October 1960, the gear-lever was cranked over for more convenient operation.

end of the crankshaft, which was too weak to withstand the pressures imposed on it. When it gave way, often after only a year's service, oil gushed onto the clutch linings, causing the clutch to slip. The solution, which took until December 1962 to effect, was to replace the oil-lubricated seal with a lubrication-free Deva metal bush.

As mentioned previously, another unfortunate problem was water intrusion – the door bins and floor regularly being filled with water the result of a stiffener joining the sill to the floorpan being lapped the wrong way. A temporary measure to cure the problem was to drill holes in the sills and fill them with expanding foam, a successful process which was carried out on completed cars at the factory. Within three months, engineers discovered the cause of the slopping water and at last remedied it by lapping the sills the correct way.

A third infamous problem was a second gear which tended to perish. This was the result of BMC's cost-cutting fitment of the gear sets and synchromesh from the Austin A35. These were simply not man enough for the job of coping with the Mini's extra gearwheels. Eventually, in October 1961, the constant-load synchromesh was replaced with baulk-ring synchromesh on the top three gears, which did at last solve the problem.

As well as having to put up with such annoyances as the water leaks, early Mini buyers suffered some raw design deficiencies, such as snapping exhausts and the fact that if the driver wore a seat belt, he could not reach the gear-lever. These were rectified piecemeal as the problems were recognized. Some, like the leaks, were resolved very quickly, but others took much longer. For instance, it was only realized that the leading edges of the lever-type door handles were dangerous when a Solihull boy was impaled on one in a freak accident. So finally, safety bosses were fitted from January 1966.

Yet the first edition of the Mini – and indeed every subsequent type – was remarkable for how little development it received. The Mini remained essentially unaltered over the entire course of its production life. Such activity as there was concentrated more on developing new variations on the Mini theme rather than trying to improve on the existing machine.

Probably the most important of the standard Mini variants was the automatic version, introduced quite late in the day in 1965. This improved the Mini's desirability as a town car, although ultimately it was not a very satisfying package: it had a disappointing fuel consumption

With the Austin Super Se7en of 1961, a more refined Mini was offered. Externally, it adopted the duo-tone paint scheme and tubular bumper extensions of the Cooper, but retained the standard Austin badge. The grille was new, incorporating vertical bars, and there were stainless steel surrounds for the front windows and steel sill finishers.

in the low-30s and was a rather dowdy performer – and this despite the 9:1 high-compression head, larger MS4 SU carburettor and revised inlet manifold to give the automatic Mini more power and torque. The four-speed AP gearbox was designed especially for the Mini and its low torque level. It was an exceptionally compact unit and was unique in that, like the manual 'box, it was lubricated by the engine's oil, not by a separate gearbox oil. Gearchanging was fully automatic, with a freewheel on first gear, and the lever was a remote Cooper-style item working on a conventional fore-and-aft gate.

With the arrival of the MkII in 1967, the Mini got the face which it retains even to this day. It also marked the arrival of 1-litre motoring in a standard Mini saloon. Even so, the changes were mainly cosmetic – and this after eight years in production. There was also considerable criticism at the time about the meagre level of fittings provided: there were still no winding windows and the same old cable-pull door handles remained. The latter were dealt with by mid-1968 and winding windows finally arrived in 1969 when extra bodyshell changes were announced (see *SECTION FOUR*).

Right from the start of the Mini's production life, the Austin facility at Longbridge was its true home. In theory, all production of Austins took place at Longbridge and the virtually identical Morrises were manufactured at Cowley, but only in saloon form. In practice, there was some cross-over: Austins sometimes emerged from Cowley and Longbridge disgorged the odd Morris. No engines were ever built at Cowley, either, and in fact many bodies and components for Morrises had to be contracted out to other suppliers. All the more specialized derivatives – from the Moke to the commercial versions and from Coopers to the Riley Elf – were built at the better-equipped Longbridge plant. It was not until 1968, following the merger of BMC with Leyland, that production was rationalized entirely at the Longbridge plant. The Cowley line was then converted and turned over to production of the new Austin Maxi.

At the same time, BLMC decided that the old policy of badge-engineering would be phased out. Its entire range of cars – not just the Mini – would be drastically rationalized over the next couple of years, witnessing the death of many venerable British marques. For the Mini, it meant the birth of a new marque: the name Mini would now be the identifying mark on the revised range. In consequence, separate Austin and Morris badges disappeared as of 1969 and the Mini entered a new era, as described in *SECTION FOUR*.

On the Super, the cord door-pulls were replaced with a lever-operated mechanism, but these proved to catch elbows so often that they only lasted a year. Also visible are the more comfortable Super seats and door trim.

Austin Se7en (1959–61) and Austin Mini MkI (1962–67)

Two badge-engineered versions of BMC's ADO15 project were launched initially in August 1959: the Morris Mini-Minor and the Austin Se7en (*sic*). The Austin name harked back to the famous prewar Seven, the first 'Baby Austin' launched in 1922. The Seven name had also been used fleetingly for the A30 at its launch in 1951. As it transpired, the Se7en name was not to last long on this model, either: it was an unwelcome and unfitting throwback to vintage times.

Two versions of the Austin Se7en were available at launch in 1959: the basic and the De Luxe, in a choice of only three colours: Farina Grey, Tartan Red and Speedwell Blue. The basic model had a very stark specification in the interests of keeping the basic price down to just £497. It had fixed rear quarter-windows, a fixed passenger seat, a bare painted millboard dash, loose rubber floor mats and cloth upholstery which was described by BMC as "rubberised hair with polyester seat cushions". There was only one sun visor, no screen washers and a bare painted filler cap.

The more upmarket De Luxe – at a premium of some £40 – had far superior trim: two-tone vinyl upholstery covering foam rubber seat cushions, flecked cockpit trim, a vinyl-covered dashboard, a chrome kick-plate on the front door pockets, carpeted front wheelarches, headlining for the rear three-quarter panels and – the luxury of it! – pile carpeting. It gained on the equipment side, too: there were standard twin screen washers, passenger seat adjustment, a passenger's sun visor, hinged rear quarter-lights, extra ashtrays and lamps in the rear side bins and a recirculatory heater/demister. In addition, the following items were chrome-plated: filler cap, rear number-plate surround and the facia switch panel surround (on the basic version, these were simply painted); in the boot, there was a rubber mat on the floor.

Externally, the De Luxe was distinguishable by its bright plastic inserts in the windscreen, rear quarter-lights and back window, its chromed filler cap, bright wheel embellishers, bright plastic finishers on the lower panel sills and front and rear bumper overriders. In practice, the Se7en De Luxe was by far the most popular choice with buyers and was effectively the 'standard' Mini.

The Austin version was distinguishable from its Morris stable-mate by its grille – eight horizontal wavy bars – and its Austin badging.

Improvements seen in the Mini-Cooper were brought to bear on a new luxury Mini, the Super Se7en, announced in September 1961 (incidentally using the same name as a Cosworth-engined Lotus launched the same year). It had a different

AUSTIN Incredible **mini** Saloon....

★ Combined ignition/starter switch.
★ Safety sun visors and interior mirror.
★ Two-leading-shoe brakes at front.
★ Greater torque capacity gearbox.

...now with Hydrolastic suspension!

In 1964, a range of changes made the Mini safer and more comfortable. The major improvement was the introduction of Issigonis' dream: Hydrolastic suspension.

Detail of the front part of the Hydrolastic suspension system. At the bottom is a rubber diaphragm, with the fluid-filled cylinder encased in a metal box. On hitting a bump, the wheel's upward movement would force fluid out of the cylinder through the hose at the top towards the corresponding rear cylinder.

slatted grille with nine wavy horizontal bars and 12 straight vertical bars, small bumper overriders front and rear, complete with nudge bars (or 'tubular extensions' as they were known). Distinguishing external trim consisted of stainless steel window surrounds and sill finishers. The Super also received duo-tone paintwork *a la* Mini-Cooper: a roof painted in contrasting white or black. Ignition was now by a combined ignition/starter key mounted in a panel in the centre of the facia. The engine was fitted with a Cooper-type 16-blade fan in place of the four-blade unit, which did such a good job of damping down engine whine that, within a month, it was fitted to all Minis.

The Super earned its luxury status with superior interior trim and extra soundproofing, with carpets in place of rubber mats, a carpet-covered wood platform in the boot, a roof-mounted interior light with its own switch, and a Cooper-style oval instrument pod containing no less than three instruments: a speedo, and water temperature and oil pressure gauges. For the first time, chromed lever-type door handles replaced the basic saloon's pull-strings, although the windows remained the sliding type. There was also a Windtone horn, adjustable seats, polyether seat cushions covered with rubberized hair trim and a black-trimmed top of the facia and a black instrument nacelle.

The Super's replacement, the Super De Luxe of October 1962, retained the chrome overriders with tubular extensions front and rear. It also gained yet another new grille, better-quality Vynide upholstery, twin sun visors mounted on chrome hinges, front ashtrays with lids, metal door pulls and kick-plates. The irksome door handles, which proved to act as hooks for passengers' clothing, were abandoned in favour of the old cord-pull type, while in the boot a rubber mat instead of carpet was given back to cover the spare wheel.

From the beginning of 1962, all models were rebadged as Austin Minis – somehow the name Mini had more of a ring to it than Seven, which had connotations of a rather remote prewar ancestry. Four-speed automatic transmission became an option from 1965, although effectively it took almost a year to reach proper production, by which time the MkII model was in sight, so few MkI automatics were made. They could be identified by their two-pedal cockpit, remote gear-lever and chrome 'Automatic' badge on the boot.

The Mini had remarkably few developments during its production life: apart from its Hydro-lastic suspension, the model remained essentially

A cutaway revealing the Mini's rear subframe. This Hydrolastic-equipped model has its fluid-filled cylinder located inboard of the rear wheel. Rear subframes were notorious for corroding in spectacular fashion.

unchanged right up until it was replaced by the Mini MkII in 1967. The simplicity and essential 'rightness' of the original dry suspension system was proven when the Mini reverted to rubber cones in 1969 (see *SECTION FOUR*).

Export models were generally badged as the Austin 850 and had numerous differences to their specifications: see *SECTION NINE: International Minis* for full details of export models.

Specification

Engine	848cc four-cylinder pushrod OHV
Engine designation	8MB
Bore/stroke	62.94 x 68.26mm
Compression ratio	8.3:1 (9:1 on automatic)
Power output	34bhp at 5,500rpm
Torque	44lb.ft at 2,900rpm (at 2,500rpm on automatic)
Transmission	Four-speed manual: Ratios: 4th 3.765, 3rd 5.317, 2nd 8.176, 1st 13.657, Rev 13.657
	Four-speed automatic option from 1965: Ratios: 4th 3.765, 3rd 5.49, 2nd 6.97, 1st 10.13, Rev 10.13
Steering	Rack & pinion
Brakes	Hydraulic drum/drum
Suspension	Independent
	Front: wishbones, rubber cones, Armstrong telescopic dampers (Hydrolastic from 1964)
	Rear: Trailing arms, rubber cones, Armstrong telescopic dampers (Hydrolastic from 1964)

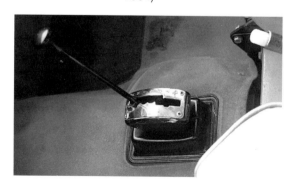

If the AP automatic gearbox was specified, a different remote lever was fitted near the front crossmember. A simple fore-and-aft movement allowed the selection of any of the four gears, or fully automatic operation.

Wheels	Pressed steel 3.5 x 10in
Tyres	5.20 x 10in Dunlop C41 cross-ply
Wheelbase	80.2in (2,036mm)
Length	120.25in (3,054mm)
Width	55in (1,397mm)
Height	53in (1,346mm)
Front track	47.375in (1,205mm)
Rear track	45.875in (1,165mm)
Weight	1,380lb (626kg)
Fuel tank	5.5gal (25l)
Luggage capacity	5.5cu ft (0.16cu m)

Performance

	Manual	Automatic
Maximum speed	75mph (120km/h)	70mph (113km/h)
0–50mph	18.3sec	18.3sec
0–60mph	29.7sec	32.0sec
30–50mph	17.5sec	19.4sec
40–60mph	24.1sec	32.1sec
50–70mph	–	–
Average fuel consumption	40mpg	33mpg

Optional extras

Recirculatory heater (for basic only)
Fresh-air heater/demister (for basic car, and on De Luxe from October 1961)
Windscreen washer (for basic only)
Overriders (for basic only)
Nudge bars (for basic and De Luxe)
Radio (for De Luxe and Super only)
Twin Windtone horns (and Alpine horns from 1964)
Foglight
Spotlight
Parking lamp (from 1964)
Wing mirrors
Mud flaps
Safety belts
Reclining seats (from 1966)
Foam rubber seats and vinyl-treated seat covers
Seat protectors and covers
Travel rugs
Felt comfykit (from 1964)
Floor carpets with underfelt (De Luxe only)
Vinyl-covered interior panels (De Luxe only)
Kick protector strips (De Luxe only)
Door pocket ashtray
Anti-mist panel
Interior bonnet release (from 1964)

Plus various non-specific BMC items, such as: reversing light, roof rack, heated rear window element, lockable fuel cap, chrome exhaust pipe deflector, supplementary instruments, auxiliary switch panel, car valeting items, touch-up paint, hand tools, cleaning fluid.

Range
Austin Se7en (1959–61)
Austin Se7en De Luxe (1959–61)
Austin Super Se7en (1961)
Austin Mini (1962–67)
Austin Mini De Luxe (1962/1964–67)
Austin Super Mini (1962)
Austin Mini Super De Luxe (1962–64)
Austin Mini Automatic (1965–67)
Austin Mini De Luxe Automatic (1965–67)

Production history
August 1959: Austin Se7en basic and De Luxe introduced (Chassis Number AA2S7 101). Cost: £497 and £537 respectively.

December 1959: Improved interior trim (Body Number 9146 – standard and 10549 – De Luxe). Also around this time, a split radiator cowl for easier access, pivoting quadrant fitted to the handbrake cable on radius arm, increased steering castor angle.

January 1960: Improved window catches for extra security (Body Number 11899).

April 1960: Driveshaft splines changed from square section to involute form (Chassis Number AA2S7 26590).

October 1960: Padding for door panels, side panels, rear parcel shelf and facia. Telescopic dampers and mountings improved and fuel tank now had drain plug. Seat belt anchorages now fitted, air cleaner changed, larger front wheel bearings fitted, clutch stop changed and gear-lever became cranked over (Chassis Number AA2S7 58698). Primary gear oil seal improved (Engine Number 16490).

May 1961: Cast-alloy suspension trumpets now fitted (Chassis Number AA2S7 123291). Key-start for high-spec models.

June 1961: Production of Super version began (first Chassis Number AA2S7S 125538).

Autumn 1961: Stronger steel wheels fitted.

September 1961: Super version launched with new grille, duo-tone paint, three-instrument oval nacelle, roof-mounted interior light and superior trim. Cost: £592.

October 1961: 16-blade fan fitted to reduce engine noise. Front grille now chrome-plated instead of painted.

January 1962: Models renamed Austin Mini (Chassis Number 197021). Larger brake cylinders fitted to all models and plastic oil filler cap on engine.

March 1962: Vynide trim replaced cloth upholstery on standard model (Chassis Number AA2S7 226055).

October 1962: De Luxe and Super discontinued and replaced by Super De Luxe, with three-gauge oval instrument pod, fresh-air heater and revised interior trim (Chassis Number AA2S7S 307125). Cost: £561. Base models now had baulk-ring synchromesh on the upper three gears and standard windscreen washer.

December 1962: Metal bush fitted to crankshaft oil seal (Engine Number 8AM UH 452359).

March 1963: More powerful heater fitted (Body Number 087448).

May 1963: Improved catch fitting for sliding windows (Body Number 091678).

February 1964: Windscreen wiper arc reduced to avoid fouling screen rubber.

September 1964: Hydrolastic suspension introduced (Chassis Number AA2S7 640203). Ignition now by key. Interior light switched by door opening as standard, oil filter warning light fitted, plus crushable sun visors and a plastic-framed driving mirror. Speedo now had white markings on black background instead of black figures on white background. Gearbox strengthened to match Cooper's (slowly introduced, then 100 per cent fit from Engine Number 8AM UH 803601). New change-speed forks, clutch now by diaphragm spring and front brakes had twin leading shoes. Super De Luxe renamed De Luxe, with vinyl-coated felt mat over spare wheel.

November 1964: Three-position driver's seat brackets.

December 1964: Stiffer rear compensating springs fitted.

January 1965: Improved scroll-type oil seal for primary gear.

October 1965: Automatic option on standard and De Luxe introduced at Motor Show, although production did not start for many months (Chassis Number AA2S7S 798693). Cost: £560 and £606 respectively.

January 1966: External door handles now had protective safety bosses (Body Number 124160). New clutch with smoother action fitted and sealed beam headlamps now standard.

October 1967: All Austin Mini MkI models replaced by new MkII.

Total production: Austin Se7en/Mini MkI saloon: approx 435,500.

Morris Mini-Minor (1959–67)

Introduced at the same time as the Austin Se7en in 1959 was the Morris Mini-Minor: tucked away in the middle of its name was the enduring tag 'Mini', which would outlast both the Austin and Morris badges by many years, eventually becoming the marque name for the car.

In almost all respects, it mirrored the specification of its sister Austin model. It, too, was available in standard and De Luxe guises, with trim differences as with the Austins. Only three colours available for the first two years, and as per tradition these were different from the Austin's: Clipper Blue, Cherry Red and Old English White. Automatic transmission was available from 1965.

The only way to tell the Morris from the Austin – apart from the badging – was the criss-cross grille, which had seven straight vertical bars and 11 straight horizontal bars. A unique option for Morris-badged Minis was that peculiar accessory of the times, whitewall tyres, although they could also be seen on the Riley Elf and Wolseley Hornet. The short-lived 1961 Super Mini-Minor model had a unique grille with 10 horizontal bars.

Many export versions of the Morris were initially known simply as the Morris 850 and Super 850. For full details of export models, see *SECTION NINE: International Minis*.

Specification
As Austin Se7en/Mini

Range
Morris Mini-Minor (1959–67)
Morris Mini-Minor De Luxe (1959–62/1964–67)
Morris Super Mini-Minor (1961–62)
Morris Mini-Minor Super De Luxe (1962–64)
Morris Mini-Minor Automatic (1965–67)
Morris Mini-Minor De Luxe Automatic (1965–67)

Optional extras
Whitewall tyres (not available for Austins)

Production history
As Austin Se7en/Mini, except:
August 1959: Morris Mini-Minor standard and De Luxe introduced (Chassis Number MA2S4 101). Cost: £497 and £537 respectively.
February 1960: Improved interior trim as per Austin of October 1960, but at Chassis Number MA2S4 14215.
April 1960: Driveshaft splines changed from square section to involute form (Chassis Number MA2S4 24831).
May 1961: Cast-alloy suspension trumpets at Chassis Number MA2S4 70376.
June 1961: Production of Super version began (first Chassis Number 125538).
September 1961: New Super model launched with unique grille with 10 horizontal bars (Chassis Number MA2S4S 75533). Cost: £592.
March 1962: Vynide trim replaced cloth upholstery on standard model (Chassis Number MA2S4 116623).
October 1962: De Luxe and Super discontinued and replaced by Super De Luxe (Chassis Number MA2S4S 148817). Cost: £561.
March 1963: More powerful heater fitted (Body Number 186267).

This is a basic version of the Morris Mini-Minor with its pared-down specification. There is a notable absence of chrome trim, and even the unique Morris grille was un-chromed, being painted white. Note the different Morris bonnet badge. *(BMIHT)*

A rear view of 'old number one', the first Mini built. Lack of a bright insert in the rear window confirms this to be a basic model.

September 1964: Hydrolastic suspension introduced (Chassis Number MA2S4 296257).

October 1965: Automatic transmission option on standard and De Luxe introduced at Earls Court Motor Show (Chassis Number MA2S4S 361001). Cost: £560 and £606 respectively.

November 1965: Safety bosses on exterior door handles (Body Number 418246).

October 1967: All MkI Morris Mini models replaced by MkII.

Total production: Morris Mini-Minor MkI saloon: approx 510,000.

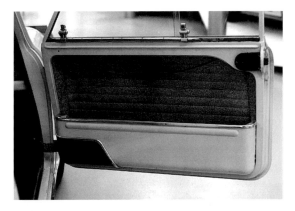

The door trim of the early Mini incorporated extremely useful door bins. Sliding windows and cord-pull door releases kept costs down.

In the rear, very useful storage bins were provided on either side, a feature retained even in today's Mini. Just how little the rear wheelarches intrude can be seen in this picture.

The 848cc engine was always built at Longbridge. The separate reservoirs for clutch and brake fluid can be seen on the left. The heater hose across the top of the engine was attached to a switchable valve in the cylinder head.

The Morris Super Mini-Minor shared the exterior brightwork additions of its Austin sister – steel front window surrounds, steel sill finishers, bumper overriders – but came with its own unique chrome grille with 10 horizontal and seven vertical bars. Note that this very early publicity car lacks the tubular bumper extensions which were standard on production cars.

Alec Issigonis with Morris Mini-Minor number one (left) and a 1965 model Mini-Minor De Luxe, which was the upmarket Mini variant. Note the chrome grille is now in the original Morris style.

Austin Se7en Countryman (1960–61), Austin Mini Countryman MkI (1962–67) and Morris Mini-Traveller MkI (1960–67)

Hot on the heels of the saloons came BMC's Austin and Morris estate cars in September 1960. While the Morris used that marque's familiar Traveller designation, Austin's version was, according to its own marque tradition, called the Se7en Countryman.

Based on the floorpan of the Mini van which had entered production in January 1960, the estate car's wheelbase was longer than the saloon's by nearly 4 inches. With the estate-type bodywork fitted, overall length was up by almost 10 inches. In keeping with the BMC marketing department's penchant for countrified 'woody' estate cars, the Countryman and Traveller came with a wooden frame glued on aft of the B-posts. Unlike previous BMC estates, notably the Morris Minor Traveller, this was a totally non-structural and purely cosmetic affectation, a fact proven by the introduction of an all-metal version to the UK market in 1962, when they undercut the 'woodies' on price by £19. The all-metal estate had been available on export markets since 1961. Some felt that a poignant remark was made about the perceived British market that BMC had bothered to develop the 'woody' at all.

The Countryman/Traveller followed the van's format of double swinging doors at the rear, hinged at the sides. The only reason this arrangement was adopted, in preference to a single opening rear door, was the most skinflint of production costings: more cars could be fitted on the production line with twin doors open than with a larger single door. More on the grounds of cost than sound planning, this arrangement would be retained until the very last Mini estates of 1982.

The layout did allow easy access to a rear load space which was cavernous by comparison with the saloon: almost seven times the volume with the seats folded at 35.3cu ft. Even with four passengers on board, 18.5cu ft of luggage could still be squeezed in, weighing up to nearly 1cwt.

The weight of the estate was 11.5cwt, about 1cwt heavier than the van, due to the extra weight of the trim. With more of the weight now carried by the rear end – a distribution of 55.4/44.6 front/rear, as compared with the saloon's 61.3/38.7 – heftier springs were fitted on the back, as per the van.

Like the van and pick-up Minis, the Countryman and Traveller were never given the Hydrolastic suspension of their saloon counterparts and the MkI was only ever available with the 848cc engine, just as the MkII would only be available with the 998cc unit.

The single trim level chosen for the estates was equivalent to the De Luxe saloon, and a pair of wing-mounted mirrors came as standard: this was a legal requirement for estate cars. However, an interior rear-view mirror was not, so this was put on the options list! Sliding rear windows were also added, which made life much more comfortable for the rear passengers than in any other

This 1959 prototype Austin Countryman shows that the basic idea of the wooden batten body was already well-formed. But there are no sliding side windows yet and the rear doors have square, not rounded backlights. Note the fancy wheeltrims, which were seen on several Mini prototypes but never saw production.

The production Austin Se7en Countryman shared many of the Van's features, but added a considerable number of its own, like sliding rear windows and folding rear passenger seats. Standard for the Countryman were twin wing mirrors; note that this car has no interior mirror, which was an optional extra.

Mini variant, especially the popular but claustrophobic budget option of buying a van and retrofitting fixed rear windows.

In the interests of presentation, the spare wheel and battery were located under the rear floor, where the van's fuel tank had been sited, so the estate cars reverted to a saloon-type fuel tank, fitted on the nearside of the rear loading bay. This had the effect of reducing the usable interior width compared with the van. At least the tank was trimmed, as were the hinged floor panels, bodysides and roof, which was not the case in the van. It was therefore a far more refined machine in all respects.

Specification
As for Austin Mini except:

Wheelbase	84.25in (2,140mm)
Length	129.9in (3,299mm)
Height	53.5in (1,360mm)
Weight	1,484lb (674kg)
Fuel tank	6.5gal (29.6l)
Luggage capacity	18.5cu ft (0.52cu m) – seats raised
	35.3cu ft (1cu m) – seats folded

Performance

Maximum speed	69mph (110km/h)
0–50mph	21.1sec
0–60mph	33.8sec
30–50mph	21.3sec
40–60mph	24.1sec
Average fuel consumption	38mpg

Optional extras
As for Austin Se7en/Mini, except:
Bumper overriders
Rear-view mirror
NB: Heated rear window not available

Range
Austin Se7en Countryman (1960–61)
Austin Mini Countryman (wooden battens) (1962–67)
Austin Mini Countryman (all-metal) (1962–67)
Morris Mini-Traveller (wooden battens) (1960–67)
Morris Mini-Traveller (all-metal) (1962–67)

Production history
March 1960: First Austin Se7en Countryman built (Chassis Number AAW7 19126).

The all-metal version of the Countryman was initially available only for export. The only difference was the deletion of the glued-on wood trim. All Mini estates were sold in only one level trim, equating to De Luxe saloon specification.

June 1960: First Morris Mini-Traveller built (Chassis Number MAW4 19101).
September 1960: Austin Se7en Countryman and Morris Mini-Traveller launched with wooden battens. Cost: £623.
April 1961: Countryman/Traveller first produced in all-metal form for export only.
January 1962: Austin version renamed Austin Mini Countryman (Chassis Number AAW7 197104).
October 1962: All-metal version of Countryman and Traveller launched in Britain alongside 'woody' (Body Number 29352 – Austin, and Chassis Number MAW4 308939 – Morris). Cost: £532. Baulk-ring synchromesh fitted on top three gears and a fresh-air heater/demister now standard.
September 1964: Ignition now by key. Interior gains oil filter change warning light, sun visor, driving mirror. Modified gearbox, diaphragm spring clutch, two leading front brake shoes (Chassis Number AAW7 639559 – Austin, and MAW4 638879 – Morris).

The wide-opening van-type rear doors allowed for easy access to a very large load area, especially with the rear seats folded.

October 1967: Traveller MkI discontinued.
November 1967: Countryman MkI discontinued.
Total production: Austin Se7en/Mini Countryman MkI: approx 85,500; Morris Mini-Traveller MkI: approx 75,500; Total: approx 161,000.

Austin Mini MkII (1967–69) and Morris Mini MkII (1967–69)

The new Mini MkII range was announced at the 1967 Motor Show at Earls Court, ushered in with the slogan: "still the incredible revolution". Once again, there were Austin and Morris versions, but the Morris was also now called simply Mini, instead of Mini-Minor.

At last there were some cosmetic changes. The front grille became more squared-up and lost the chrome lips extending towards the sides: a thicker enveloping chrome surround was fitted instead. There were still distinguishing grilles for the Austin and Morris versions, however: the Austin acquired an 11-bar grille, while the Morris had 13 horizontal bars and seven vertical ones. The saloon's rear window became larger and the new squarish rear light clusters were larger in size,

too. There were new 'MkII' badges for the tail.

It was not all froth, however. The turning circle was significantly reduced from 32ft to 28ft by increasing the number of teeth on the steering rack and slightly lengthening the steering arms. The brakes were improved with increased bores on the front and rear slave cylinders, which made pedal action lighter.

Yet the biggest news was the availability of the 998cc engine in the standard saloon bodyshell. The 1-litre engine was the same as the one fitted to the Riley Elf, Wolseley Hornet and which also formed the basis of the Mini-Cooper's. This gave the Minis a useful new turn of speed. In contrast with the 850 model, the 1000 received the Cooper-type remote gearchange and higher 3.44:1 final-drive ratio. Automatic transmission remained available as an option on all models, which continued to have the higher-compression 9:1 engine with the SU HS4 carburettor. The AP automatic gearbox progressed to an improved MkII specification, as ever its inclusion distinguished by a chrome badge on the boot.

As before, there was a hierarchy in the Mini range. The 850 model came in two guises: basic and Super De Luxe. The latter was distinguished by the chrome surround to the windows, the hinged rear quarter-lights, the three-instrument oval nacelle, restyled seats with a better shape, a

standard heater and carpets. It no longer had the wraparound overriders of the MkI Super De Luxe, which were inappropriate for the new, larger rear lights. The 1000 model was only available in Super De Luxe form. An identifying chrome badge reading '850' or '1000' on the lower right-hand side of the bootlid denoted which engine was fitted.

Inside, the old instrument binnacles were retained (single-dial in the basic 848cc Mini, three-dial in all other versions), with the speedo and oil gauge – when fitted – marked with additional metric readings. The dials also gained safer bezels. The switchgear was moved forward by 3 inches, which finally allowed passengers wearing the – still optional – seat belts to operate them without unbuckling. A foam-filled roll was also added across the dash for safety reasons. The (louder) horn and indicators were now grouped on a single stalk and the indicators gained an audio warning signal; the flashing warning light was relocated from the end of the stalk to a position on the speedo. The floor-mounted dipswitch finally gave way to a headlamp flasher located on the indicator/horn stalk and the windscreen wipers were at last self-parking.

In September 1968, all Minis were finally given the all-synchromesh four-speed gearbox first seen in the Cooper S in October 1967.

Following the merger of BMC with the truck giant Leyland, a period of rationalization took place and production of the Mini at the Cowley works ceased, all production then being concentrated at the Austin works at Longbridge: For a time during this transitional period, Austin Minis could come with Morris hubcaps, and Morris Minis sometimes had Austin versions!

The MkII Mini models lasted two years, badged as Austin and Morris. In the light of the momentous changes sweeping through BLMC, the era of badge-engineering was coming to a close. Concurrent with the launch of the new Mini Clubman, the name Mini was adopted as the single marque name for almost all Mini derivatives from 1969. The familiar Mini body-shell was not, of course, ousted by the arrival of the Clubman, but continued as the Mini 850 and 1000 with dry-cone suspension from November 1969. For this era of the Mini's life, see *SECTION FOUR*.

The Mini's rear end was significantly altered in the MkII: the rear screen was larger, as were the new-shape rear-light clusters. There was new badging on the bootlid, too: this Austin version has 'Austin' script flanked by the words 'Mini' and 'MkII', plus an engine-identifying chrome badge to the lower left. This automatic version also has an identifying badge below the boot handle.

Specification

	Mini 850 MkII	Mini 1000 MkII
Engine	848cc OHV four-cylinder	998cc OHV four-cylinder
Engine designation	8MB, 8AH with auto 'box	99H, 9AG with auto 'box
Bore/stroke	62.94 x 68.26mm	64.59 x 76.2mm
Compression ratio	8.3:1 (9:1 auto 'box)	8.3:1 (9:1 auto 'box)
Power output	34bhp at 5,500rpm	38bhp at 5,250rpm
Torque	44lb.ft at 2,900rpm	52lb.ft at 2,700rpm
Transmission	Four-speed manual	Four-speed manual
	Ratios: see MkI	Ratios: 4th 3.44, 3rd 4.86,
		2nd 7.47, 1st 12.48
	Four-speed auto option	Four-speed auto option
Steering	Rack & pinion	Rack & pinion
Brakes	Hydraulic drum/drum	Hydraulic drum/drum
Suspension	Independent	Independent
	Hydrolastic	Hydrolastic
Wheelbase	80.2in (2,036mm)	80.2in (2,036mm)
Length	120.25in (3,054mm)	120.25in (3,054mm)
Width	55.5in (1,410mm)	55.5in (1,410mm)
Height	53in (1,346mm)	53in (1,346mm)
Front track	47.4in (1,204mm)	47.4in (1,204mm)
Rear track	45.9in (1,166mm)	45.9in (1,166mm)
Weight	1,395lb (634kg)	1,400lb (636kg)
Fuel tank	5.5gal (25l)	5.5gal (25l)
Luggage capacity	5.5cu ft (0.15cu m)	5.5cu ft (0.15cu m)

Performance

Maximum speed	74mph (118km/h)	75mph (120km/h)
0–50mph	18.3sec	17.2sec
0–60mph	29.7sec	26.2sec
30–50mph	17.5sec	13.7sec
40–60mph	24.1sec	18.8sec
50–70mph	–	–
Average fuel consumption	40mpg	34mpg

Morris versions had a similar new rear badge with the Morris symbol flanked by the words 'Morris' and 'Mini MkII'.

The Austin Mini Super De Luxe was sold in 850 and 1000 forms. Much the same distinguishing features persisted between this and the basic model: bright front and rear screen surrounds, wheeltrims, hinged rear quarter-lights, bumper over-riders and superior interior fitments.

Optional extras

Fresh-air heater (basic model only)
Automatic transmission
Reclining front seats (until January 1969)
Rake-adjustable front seats (from January 1969)
Electrically heated rear window (from April 1969)
Seat belts

Range

Austin Mini MkII 850 (1967–69)
Austin Mini MkII 850 Super De Luxe (1967–69)
Austin Mini MkII 1000 Super De Luxe (1967–69)
Morris Mini MkII 850 (1967–69)
Morris Mini MkII 850 Super De Luxe (1967–69)
Morris Mini MkII 1000 Super De Luxe (1967–69)

The old-style Morris chrome grille was retained within the new MkII's squarish surround. This is a Super De Luxe version.

Production history

October 1967: Austin and Morris Mini MkII introduced, both marques offered in 850 basic, 850 Super De Luxe and 1000 Super De Luxe versions (Chassis Number A/A2SB 1068001 – Austin, and M/A2S6 507001 – Morris). Cost: £509, £555 and £579 respectively.

November 1967: Moulded plastic cooling fan fitted.

1968: All Mini production transferred to Longbridge.

June 1968: Internal door handles replaced cable-pull releases.

August 1968: All-synchromesh gearbox standard on 1000 models.

September 1968: All-synchromesh gearbox standard on 850 models (Engine Number 8AM WE H 101).

April 1969: Heated rear window available as an option.

October 1969: Final Austin 850 Super De Luxe and Austin 1000 Super De Luxe produced.

November 1969: All models officially replaced by Mini 850 and Mini 1000. Final Morris 850 standard produced.

December 1969: Final Austin 850 standard produced (Chassis Number A/A2SB 1372023). Final Morris 850 Super De Luxe and Morris 1000 Super De Luxe produced (final Chassis Number M/A2S6 713901).

Total production: Austin Mini MkII saloon: approx 154,000; Morris Mini MkII saloon: approx 206,000; Total: 360,000.

Austin Mini Countryman MkII and Morris Mini-Traveller MkII (1967–69)

At the same time as changes were made to the Mini saloons, so the estate versions were given the MkII treatment. This included the new grilles – in distinct Austin and Morris versions – and all the same mechanical improvements. All-synchromesh gears arrived in 1968 and there was always an automatic gearbox option. Yet the rear windows remained the same as before, and the rear light clusters were also unaltered from MkI specification. Once again, both wooden-framed and all-metal types were offered alongside each other.

The big difference over the MkI was the fitment of the 998cc engine in place of the 848cc unit. The small increase in power and torque better suited the load-carrying duties of the little all-rounder. Not only the Austin and Morris badges were lost when production ended at the end of 1969: both the Countryman and Traveller names were also dropped. Their replacement was the Mini Clubman Estate, which many regarded as something of a retrograde step. This event also marked the end of the wooden-batten Mini estate car.

The Austin Mini Countryman MkII shared the front end modifications of the saloon, although its rear end remained the same as before. Both wooden and all-metal versions continued to be offered, both of them with the 998cc engine only.

Specification

As Mini MkII 1000, except:

Suspension	Independent by rubber cones
Wheelbase	84.25in (2,140mm)
Length	129.9in (3,299mm)
Height	53.5in (1,360mm)
Weight	1,455lb (660kg)
Fuel tank	6.5gal (29.6l)
Luggage capacity	18.5cu ft (0.52cu m)
	– seats raised
	35.3cu ft (1cu m)
	– seats folded

Performance

As Mini MkII 1000

Optional extras

As Saloon, except:
Fresh-air heater standard
Heated rear window not available

Range

Austin Mini Countryman MkII 1000 (wooden battens) (1967–69)

Austin Mini Countryman MkII 1000 (all-metal) (1967–69)
Morris Mini-Traveller MkII 1000 (wooden battens) (1967–69)
Morris Mini-Traveller MkII 1000 (all-metal) (1967–69)

Production history

October 1967: Austin Mini Countryman MkII 1000 and Morris Mini-Traveller MkII 1000 introduced (Chassis Number A/AWB 1068101- Austin, and M/AW6 1068401). Cost: £610 (all-metal) and £629 (wooden battens).
August 1968: All-synchromesh gearbox fitted (Engine Number 99H 159 H 101).
October 1969: Final Austin Mini Countryman manufactured (Chassis Number A/AWB 1359152).
November 1969: Final Morris Mini-Traveller manufactured (Chassis Number M/AW6 1368676).
Total production: Austin Mini Countryman MkII: approx 22,500; Morris Mini-Traveller MkII: approx 23,500; Total: 46,000.

The Morris Mini-Traveller, with its distinctive MkII grille to distinguish it from its Austin counterpart, proved to be slightly the more popular of the two Mini estates before they were replaced by a common model with Clubman styling at the end of 1969. (BMIHT)

The Mini-Cooper

While the Mini was slowly but surely becoming the 'people's car' which Alec Issigonis had always intended it to be, it was the Mini-Cooper which would become the enduring legend in the history of the Mini. Inextricably linked with racing and rallying, the Mini-Cooper was also one of the most exciting road cars of its day. To many, it is still the ultimate Mini.

The idea of a performance Mini was quite alien to Issigonis. His goal had been to create minimal transport and he baulked at the notion of dressed-up Minis of any sort: he fought the introduction of wooden battens on the Mini estate cars, unsuccessfully, and his reservations about a go-fast Mini were equally unsuccessful.

The man behind the birth of the Mini-Cooper was John Cooper, the successful racing car manufacturer whose cars triumphed in the Formula 1 World Championships of 1959 and 1960. His exploits in the Formula Junior world included using the BMC A-series engine and he eventually took on BMC's works Formula Junior team. Naturally, he got to know Alec Issigonis and, of course, ADO15 – the Mini.

As soon as Cooper tried a prototype Mini, he was very struck by it and was convinced that it had huge competition potential. He thought it would make an ideal Touring Car competitor and immediately suggested that a run of 1000 1-litre-engined Minis be built to homologate them for racing. Issigonis was not interested, but Cooper managed to persuade Sir George Harriman, head of BMC, to give the go-ahead. Everyone appreciated the Mini's potential, and the further success of privately converted Minis in racing events was enough to convince BMC that it ought to offer its own high-performance version. The project was given the go-ahead with the code name ADO50.

By increasing the stroke of the A-series engine, Cooper was already getting amazing results in his Formula Junior engines: he had extracted up to 83bhp from the most powerful units. However, for the roadgoing Mini-Cooper, it was thought that 55bhp would be quite enough to get the little car up to a target maximum speed of 85mph.

So the 848cc engine was stroked from 68.26mm to 81.28mm. In order to maintain flexibility and prevent weaknesses, the bore was reduced from 62.94mm to 62.43mm, giving an overall increase

Coopers ancient and modern: a 1967 Mini-Cooper face to face with Rover's 1990 version. The grilles may look the same, but a huge catalogue of changes separated the years.

The first Austin Se7en Cooper externally resembled the Super Se7en, but that belied the Cooper's major changes under the skin. The new 997cc A-series engine developed 55bhp, taking it to 87mph. Front disc brakes improved the stopping power.

in cylinder volume of 17.5 per cent to 997cc. The tops of the pistons were domed to raise the compression ratio from 8.3:1 to 9:1 and the inlet valve areas were slightly increased. The exhaust bore was also a little wider and the manifold was changed to a three-way unit. A higher-lift camshaft was developed, using larger inlet valves and double valve springs.

With twin 1.25in SU carburettors fitted, the power output shot up to the target 55bhp, developed at 6,000rpm. Because of the higher revs which would be encountered with the new engine, a damper was fitted on the engine to reduce vibrational wear on the timing gears and an oilway was drilled into the crank and bearings. It was also felt that the bottom end of the engine should be strengthened to withstand the extra power. To combat earlier criticisms of the Mini's buzz-box engine noise, a 16-blade fan was installed instead of the four-blade type.

Remote gearchanges were already being offered by aftermarket specialists for the standard Mini and it was felt that spirited gearchanging would make a remote shift essential in the Mini-Cooper. At the same time, the gear ratios were lengthened to make better use of the increased power and torque, and the final drive was raised to 3.765:1. The intermediate gear speeds at 6,000rpm – as marked on the speedo – were 28, 47 and 72mph, as compared with 23, 38 and 58mph in the 848cc Mini. The Mini-Cooper's top speed was a remarkable 87.4mph, as tested by *The Autocar*.

To cope with the extra power, John Cooper persuaded Lockheed to develop a special front disc brake set-up for the Mini's tiny 10-inch wheels – a pioneering development. The 7in discs certainly did the job of stopping the Mini-

Cooper, being quite a revelation in their day. Although by today's standards, the front discs are not up to much – and they were considerably enhanced in the forthcoming Cooper 'S' – their servo-assisted stopping power was a big advance over the standard Mini's drums. Rear drums were retained, albeit with an uprated pressure-limiting valve.

John Cooper came to an arrangement with BMC whereby his name would be used on the new performance Mini in return for a royalty paid on each car sold. The agreement worked well: BMC brought the kudos of Cooper's name to its products and John Cooper must have made a tidy sum over the 10 years that the deal lasted.

BMC planned to show the new Mini-Cooper to the press at a private function in July 17, 1961, and as late as a week before the scheduled date there was still not one car fully-finished to show them. With some relief, the BMC engineers just made their deadline.

The Mini-Cooper was publicly launched in September 1961, with the advertising line 'For Superformance'. It received rapturous praise. *The Autocar* called it "an astonishingly fast means of reaching B from A", and *The Motor* concluded: "This is the fastest production saloon of its size ever to figure in our road test reports...a sum of about £680 is better spent on this model than on something bigger but no better". It was the extra in-gear acceleration which most impressed the testers, particularly in the 40–70mph range.

The brakes were much-praised, as was the handling. The Cooper still understeered – in fact, more so than the standard Mini because of the additional cornering forces, but it was more controllable. By simply adjusting right-foot pedal pressure to the required degree most of the effects of understeer could be cancelled.

The Cooper was immediately identifiable by its duo-tone paintwork. It was decidedly not a stripped-out racer, but slotted in as the top-of-the-range model. Hence, it received most of the superior trim and fittings developed for the Super Mini, which was launched contemporaneously with the Cooper. The new Mini-Cooper was perhaps an expensive buy at £679 7s 3d, but the sheer volume of sales it attracted testifies to the success of BMC's market strategy: almost one in five Mini sales within a year of launch were Coopers.

The enthusiastic reception for the Cooper was more than matched by its competition exploits, which flowed thick and fast. BMC knew they had a winner on their hands. Very quickly, the Cooper became *the* car to have. The works team fielded Rauno Aaltonen in the 1962 Monte Carlo Rally, where he moved up to second place before overturning. Then Pat Moss and Ann Wisdom won the Tulip Rally and the Mini-Cooper had scored its first of many works rally victories. In the British Saloon Car Championship, the Coopers all but cleaned up. The 997cc Mini-Cooper's last major success was at the 1963 Tulip Rally with Paddy Hopkirk at the wheel, when it came first in its class and second in the Touring Car class irrespective of capacity. However, it was the Mini-Cooper 'S' which was to sweep all before it and carve the Mini's mark indelibly on motor racing history.

Even Alec Issigonis' imagination had been fired by the success of the Mini-Cooper, such that he collaborated with John Cooper in developing the legendary Mini-Cooper 'S', the 'S' nominally standing for Sport. With Stuart Turner as BMC's new competition manager, development of the Cooper 'S' was given enthusiastic support. This was a car which BMC hoped would improve on the standard Cooper's impressive competition record – and succeed it did, in spectacular fashion.

Much of the development work for the 'S' was carried out by consultant specialists working closely with the competition department at Abingdon. Notably this involved Daniel Richmond of Downton Engineering, who worked rigorously to the requirements demanded by Issigonis.

With more than an eye on competition, it was decided to go back to the 848cc engine and develop a more powerful unit from basics. The 1,100cc class in motorsport was waning in importance as most of the major formulae were now operating to 1,000cc and 1,300cc limits. To take advantage of both, it was decided to develop an engine to the old 1,100cc formula which could then be long or short-stroked to the required limits. Besides, BMC and John Cooper had far more experience with the 1,100cc class than either of the others.

Hence the original stroke of 68.26mm was retained, while the bore was taken out to just about its feasible limit at 70.6mm, a rare example of an oversquare A-series engine. This gave a capacity of 1,071cc and this engine became the first to be offered in the new Mini-Cooper 'S'. Keeping the same bore would allow the long and short-stroke engines to be manufactured using essentially the same block, with only different-throw crankshafts to fit on the production lines.

The changes to the 'S' series engine were far-reaching. The new crankshaft was made from

The Austin Se7en Cooper could be distinguished from its Super sister by its 'Austin Cooper' badging and a new grille with 11 chrome slats and two vertical bars. Duo-tone paint schemes provided the classic Cooper appearance.

high-quality EN40B steel, which was nitride-hardened; the big-end bearings were 2 inches in diameter. Further, there were enlarged oil bores and a high-pressure competition oil pump, while the rockers were forged rather than pressed and the inlet and exhaust valves were considerably larger. The valve guides were also made of a strong and expensive cupro-nickel alloy called Nimonic 80, and the valves themselves had welded-on stellite faces which better resisted rocker wear.

Both the block and the head of the 'S' engines looked different from the normal 848cc A-series units. The head could be identified by its extra securing nut and bolt. In the block, the outer two cylinder bores were moved further apart, while the inner two moved slightly closer together, producing an engine which dispensed with the tappet side-cover familiar on other A-series engines (with the exception of the 1,275cc).

The 1,071cc Mini-Cooper 'S' appeared in March 1963. Its engine was naturally the highlight of the testers' praise. It used the same camshaft as the standard Mini-Cooper with that specially Nitrided steel crank and enhanced conrods. Fitted with twin 1.25in SU carburettors,

the outcome was a maximum power output of 70bhp at 6,200rpm, although the engine was designed to rev right up to 7,200rpm.

The net result of the modifications was a heady turn of speed for the new Mini: *The Motor* recorded a top speed of 94.5mph and 0–60mph in 12.9 seconds – impressive stuff indeed for 1963, so much so that the magazine was stirred to call it "astonishing". It was not just the ultimate performance which impressed: the engine had a wide-based torque curve, offering tractable and surprisingly docile characteristics.

The standard transmission was the same as that in the normal Cooper: a 3.765:1 final drive with intermediate ratios of 5.1, 7.21 and 12.04:1. A 3.44:1 final drive was an optional fitment, as was a close-ratio gearbox. This could be specified with either final drive. Thus the 'S' could be tailored to a variety of demands, from enthusiastic road use to full-blown rallying.

Braking had to be improved to deal with the higher performance of the 'S', so thicker and wider diameter front discs were fitted: they were now up from 0.25in to 0.375in thick and from 7in to 7.5in across. This greatly enhanced braking efficiency and made the discs 80 per cent more

While it took a few months for the Austin to be called a Mini-Cooper, the Morris version was known as a Mini-Cooper from the start. It had its own unique grille with seven chrome slats and different Morris marque badging.

The 998cc Cooper engine looked little different from the early 997cc unit, but it delivered a more flexible power output and so provided better performance.

resistant to heat damage. Tougher pads and linings, Hydrovac servo-assistance and a revised rear brake pressure-limiting valve completed the picture. To aid cooling, the 'S' was also given ventilated steel wheels and Dunlop radial tyres were standard. Finally, the steering was given a higher ratio (2.3 turns lock-to-lock), making it a more manoeuvrable machine.

The Cooper 'S' was aimed squarely at the well-to-do enthusiast with a bent for racing or rallying. Hence, BMC offered a range of options to suit possible use in competition. In addition to the gearbox options, a second fuel tank, a sump guard, wider 4.5in rims and an oil cooler could also eventually be specified.

In competition, the 'S' made an immediate impression. Paddy Hopkirk won the Touring Car class and came third overall in the 1963 Tour de France with the now-famous early 1071S, registered 33 EJB. The same car and driver went on to score the first of a historic series of victories in the 1964 Monte Carlo Rally. Minis picked up the team prize in the same event. Such competition victories undoubtedly did much to bolster Mini sales in Britain and the whole of Europe and laid the foundations of the Cooper legend which was to flower fully with the 1275S.

The 1071S was originally intended to be built in a run of just 1,000 cars to homologate it for International Touring Car racing and it only remained in production for one year. However, during this time, just over 4,000 were actually built, and some reckon the original 1071S engine to be the sweetest of all the Cooper 'S' variants.

By March 1964, when the last 1071S was built, the long and short-stroke versions of the same car were just about production-ready. Prototypes had sampled racing experience during the previous year and the obsolescence of the 1,100cc racing class brought them forward. There were two engine sizes: 970cc (which was put into production solely to homologate the model for racing) and 1,275cc, which broke cover first in April 1964 and became the definitive Cooper 'S'.

The engine developed for the 1275S was essentially the same as the 1,071cc unit, but stroked to 81.33mm, or almost as much as the original 997cc Mini-Cooper. That gave a total capacity of 1,275cc. To cope with the longer stroke, the cylinder block needed to be slightly taller.

However, the results were magnificent. The 1275S engine punched out a healthy 76bhp at 5,800rpm and was by far the most torquey of all the Mini-Cooper engines, with no less than 80lb.ft at 3,000rpm. It was strong, versatile and, in the long-run, reliable. It was also to have a far larger significance in the fortunes of BMC and BL: it was the basis for the 1,275cc A-series engine which became the backbone of BL's small car programme during the Seventies, including other Minis – although none had the same charisma and 'oomph' as the Cooper 1275S.

The best early road test of a 1275S was *Autosport*'s. John Bolster succeeded in reaching 'the ton', with a scorching 0–60mph time of only 9 seconds. *Motor* commented that: "Two thousand pounds [when the 1275S cost £778] will

The Cooper's dashboard was the same as the Super's, with the distinctive oval instrument nacelle. However, the speedo was calibrated to 100mph and the gearbox was operated by a remote lever. Seat coverings were unique to the Cooper.

Later 998cc-engined MkI Coopers had longer toggle switches and a 105mph speedometer. The change-up points are marked at 28, 45 and 64mph on the inner circumference. Note the patterned brocade trim.

not buy a sportscar that makes shorter work of cross-country journeys on indifferent roads". BMC's 'recommended' maximum in-gear times for its ultimate Mini were 33, 54 and 78mph.

In its shadow, the short-stroke 970S took something of a back seat. The 970cc engine was realized by shortening the stroke to 61.9mmm, by far the shortest of any A-series engine. This allowed it to rev very freely and sweetly, and the 970S was perhaps better to drive than any other 'S'. Yet its power output and, in particular, its maximum torque were significantly below those of the 1275S. The engines were comparatively expensive to make and the 970S was only ever available to special order.

Yet it allowed BMC to homologate the model in the 1,000cc class, and it built just enough to do so (a fraction short of 1,000 examples) in a mere seven months. To its credit, the 970S remained competitive in racing for many years, although after the end of the homologation period, many 970S Coopers were converted to different A-series engines, making the original 970cc car a genuine rarity today.

Meanwhile, the 1275S dramatically continued the earlier competition successes of the 1071S. Timo Makinen scored a second win for the Cooper in the 1965 Monte Carlo Rally and the same year saw Makinen win the 1000 Lakes – one of a series of four wins for him in this event – while Rauno Aaltonen won the European Rally

Championship and RAC Rally and Paddy Hopkirk took his third successive Circuit of Ireland. Mini-Coopers were sweeping the board, not only in rallies, but in circuit racing, club events and even autocross. In 1966, Mini-Coopers took the first three places in the Monte Carlo Rally, only to be disqualified on a highly controversial technical infringement. That prevented the Cooper scoring a historic three wins in succession in the Monte, but BMC had gained all the publicity it needed to make the Mini-Cooper 'S' a motoring legend.

However, slowly but surely, advances made by other manufacturers began to eat away the Minis' domination in motorsports. Their reliability kept them in good stead despite their increasing uncompetitiveness, but the nail in the coffin was the cost-cutting post-BLMC regime presided over by Sir Donald Stokes which amongst other measures saw the works rally team have the plug pulled on it in 1968.

The roadgoing Mini-Coopers, meanwhile, received most of the product developments gained by the rest of the Mini range. Naturally, the introduction of Hydrolastic suspension to all Mini saloons included the Coopers. BMC's line for the all-elastic Coopers went: "More controlled cornering, firmer roadholding and an even smoother ride". Well, that may have been true, but enthusiasts recognized that there were shortcomings in the system for a performance-orientated car. Magazine tests bemoaned the extra roll of the fluid-sprung Mini-Cooper, even if its handling was ultimately unaffected. The pitching effect brought on by Hydrolastic was disliked by many, especially in the competition world, and a high proportion of competition Coopers were returned to dry rubber-cone suspension. Others simply used the way the nose bobbed according to the acceleration load to their own advantage by 'jumping' obstacles in the road surface using their right foot!

Unlike other Minis, which reverted to dry-cone suspension from late 1969, the Mini-Cooper 'S' continued to be fitted with Hydrolastic suspension right up until 1971, simply to use up the supply of left-over parts. Yet a handful of the very last of the Cooper 'S' models may have been built with rubber cones after Hydrolastic finally ran out.

The Mini-Cooper was often treated to items of equipment well before they became available on ordinary Minis. The remote gearchange was one example, and others included the three-gauge instrument nacelle and the availability of reclining seats from 1965.

It was the Stokes regime which eventually killed the Mini-Cooper. First, the standard Cooper was replaced by the 1275 GT in 1969, which many regarded as a retrograde step. Stokes' official explanation was that the Cooper name was attracting too high insurance premiums – and then the 1275 GT was promptly placed in the same category!

The demise of the Mini-Cooper came about more as a result of cost-cutting and rationalization at British Leyland. The diversity of Mini models was being pared down such that there would only

Coopers had the luxury of a carpeted wooden platform in the boot, supported by metal towers. This covered the spare wheel and battery and could be removed for access.

be five varieties by 1971. However, the notion of paying John Cooper a royalty of some £2 on each Mini-Cooper sold eventually rankled BL so that its agreement was withdrawn in August 1971, exactly 10 years after the first Mini-Cooper was built. The only car which could hope to be a successor was the Mini 1275 GT, but everyone except BLMC's public relations department thought it was a very poor substitute. The Cooper magic had gone.

Almost without exception, all Mini-Coopers, both Austin and Morris, were built at Longbridge, the major exceptions being several foreign-built Coopers. BMC Australia built CKD kit Coopers for many years; Innocenti produced their own Mini-Cooper until 1974; and Spanish-built Coopers were made by the firm AUTHI. For details, see *SECTION NINE: International Minis*.

The final chapter in the Cooper story is still being written. John Cooper, who went on to open his own garage, ended up happily converting Minis to 'Mini-Coopers' from 1985. Following support from Japan, where the Mini – and especially the Cooper – is held in semi-deistic esteem, the Rover Group was finally persuaded that it should offer a Mini-Cooper once again, which it did from 1990. Reference to that part of the Mini-Cooper story will be found in *SECTION FOUR*.

Austin Se7en Cooper, Austin and Morris Mini-Cooper 997cc and 998cc MkI (1961–64/1964–67)

The Austin Se7en Cooper and Morris Mini-Cooper were announced at the same time as the Super Mini in September 1961, but were intended to be the top-of-the-range performance versions. As such, they became the first Minis to be fitted with an engine of more than 848cc, sporting a reduced-bore but longer-stroke engine of 997cc capacity. It had twin SU HS2 carburettors fitted with GZ needles and came with a nine-stud cylinder head bearing the casting number 12G185.

Mechanically, the new Mini-Cooper differed from standard Minis mainly in having front disc brakes and a higher final-drive close-ratio gearbox with a remote change. There were wider Dunlop tyres, which improved roadholding.

The Mini-Cooper was distinguishable externally from the standard Mini in several respects: the most striking was the famous duo-tone paint scheme, with the main body in one colour and the roof in a contrasting colour, which would become the hallmark of Mini-Coopers and would quickly be copied by owners of standard Minis. Incidentally, there was never a red-and-white paint scheme for road cars: that was reserved only for the works team models. Roadgoing Coopers with red paintwork always came with a black roof, as did white cars. All other colours (blue, green, grey and yellow) were supplied with a white roof.

Once again, there were Austin and Morris variants. Initially, the Austin was called the Se7en Cooper, but within five months it, too, was called a Mini-Cooper. There was a unique grille for each: the Austin version had 11 chromed horizontal slats, while the Morris had only seven. Apart from Austin and Morris badges – which read 'Austin Cooper' and 'Morris Cooper' – there was nothing else to separate the models. On both, the front bumper was of the type developed in parallel for the Mini Super, launched simultaneously with the Cooper, with its standard overriders and nudge bars.

Inside, there was a concerted effort to make the Cooper the top of the range, with trim largely shared with the Super. A new vinyl-coated material covered the dashboard, there was two-tone leathercloth upholstery, a fully-carpeted floor and the boot had an estate-type carpeted wood platform over the spare wheel. The central instrument pod was expanded to become an ovoid containing no less than three Smiths gauges: a central speedometer – calibrated to 100mph and with a five-digit odometer – a water temperature gauge to the left of it and an oil pressure gauge to the right. The switchable interior courtesy lamp moved from the instrument panel to the roof as a result of the new panel.

Like the Austin version, the Morris Mini-Cooper began life with a 997cc engine before switching to a twin-carburettor development of the 998cc unit fitted to the Riley Elf and Wolseley Hornet. This had a larger bore and a shorter stroke and offered more stamina at high revs. (BMIHT)

The major change during the MkI Mini-Cooper's life was the fitment in 1964 of the same capacity 998cc engine as the Riley Elf and Wolseley Hornet, but with twin carburettors to give 55bhp at 5,800rpm, thus providing slightly superior performance. The addition of just one extra cubic centimetre might not seem much, but the 998cc unit was a quite different engine. It was a natural choice in terms of production logistics, bringing it into line with the existing Riley/Wolseley engine production and eliminating the need to build a special Cooper unit. The twin SU HS2 carbs were retained, but were now fitted with GY needles. Both high and low-compression versions were offered, both with the casting number 12G295 on the nine-stud cylinder head.

There was no brake servo in the 998, but it had a smaller-bore master-cylinder and a larger-volume fluid reservoir. The 998's trim did not change significantly over the 997, although there was a previously-unavailable option of reclining front seats from 1965.

In 1964, the Cooper was produced with the same Hydrolastic suspension system fitted simultaneously to all Mini saloons. It was superseded by the Mini-Cooper MkII in October 1967.

Specification

	Mini-Cooper 997	Mini-Cooper 998
Engine	997cc 4-cyl OHV	998cc 4-cyl OHV
Engine designation	9F	9FA/9FD
Bore/stroke	62.43 x 81.28mm	64.6 x 76.2mm
Compression ratio	9:1	High comp: 9:1
		Low comp: 7.8:1
Power output	55bhp at 6,000rpm	55bhp at 5,800rpm
Torque	54.5lb.ft at 3,600rpm	High: 57lb.ft at 3,000rpm;
		Low: 56lb.ft at 2,900rpm
Transmission	Four-speed manual: Ratios: 4th 3.765, 3rd 5.11, 2nd 7.21, 1st 12.05, Optional 3.44:1 final drive	
Steering	Rack and pinion	
Brakes	Hydraulic disc/drum	
Suspension	Independent	
	Front: Wishbones, rubber cones, Armstrong telescopic dampers (Hydrolastic from 1964)	
	Rear: Trailing arms, rubber cones, Armstrong telescopic dampers (Hydrolastic from 1964)	
Wheels	Pressed steel 3.5 x 10in	
Tyres	Dunlop SP3 5.20-10in radial-ply (to 1964)	
	Dunlop SP41 145-10in radial-ply tubeless (from 1964)	
Wheelbase	80in (2,032mm)	
Length	120.25in (3,054mm)	
Width	55in (1,397mm)	
Height	53in (1,346mm)	
Front track	47.75in (1,213mm)	
Rear track	45.9in (1,166mm)	
Weight	1,400lb (636kg)	
Fuel tank	5.5gal (25l)	
Luggage capacity	5.5cu ft (0.15cu m)	

Performance

Maximum speed	87mph (140km/h)	90mph (145km/h)
0–50mph	12.6sec	11.9sec
0–60mph	18.0sec	16.8sec
30–50mph	12.6sec	11.3sec
40–60mph	13.3sec	12.1sec
50–70mph	16.7sec	15.1sec
Average fuel consumption	27mpg	33mpg

Optional extras

3.44:1 final-drive ratio (until 1964)
Close-ratio gearbox (from 1964)
Fresh-air heater (standard from 1962)
Radio
Anti-mist panel
Wing mirrors
Laminated windscreen
Car valeting items
Seat belts
Reclining front seats (from 1965)
Heated rear window (from 1967)
Touch-up paint
Auxiliary lamps
Switch panel for auxiliary equipment
Hand tools
Rubber mats

Range

Austin Se7en Cooper (1961)
Austin Mini-Cooper 997cc (1962–64)
Austin Mini-Cooper 998cc (1964–67)
Morris Mini-Cooper 997cc (1961–64)
Morris Mini-Cooper 998cc (1964–67)

Production history

July 1961: Austin Se7en Cooper and Morris Mini-Cooper first produced (Chassis Number C/A2S7 138301 – Austin, and K/A2S4 138311 – Morris).
September 1961: Official public launch of Austin Se7en Cooper and Morris Mini-Cooper, identical but for grilles and badges. Cost: £679.
January 1962: Austin Se7en Cooper now known as Austin Mini-Cooper.
July 1962: Baulk-ring synchromesh introduced.
March 1963: Superior front disc brakes fitted (Chassis Number C/A2S7 382832 – Austin, and K/A2S4 382183 – Morris). More powerful heater standard (Body Number 013823).
May 1963: Better window catches fitted (Body Number 015069). Aluminium suspension trumpets instead of steel (Chassis Number C/A2S7 401300 – Austin, and K/A2S4 4000370 – Morris).
September 1963: Improved telescopic dampers (Chassis Number C/A2S7 463437 – Austin, and K/A2S4 462234 – Morris).
November 1963: First 998cc engines produced.
January 1964: 997cc engine discontinued (final Chassis Numbers C/A2S7 489222 – Austin, and K/A2S4 487907 – Morris). Replaced with new 998cc engine with prefix 9FA (Chassis Number C/A2S7 502447 – Austin, K/A2S4 502482 – Morris).

February 1964: Wiper arc reduced.
March 1964: Dunlop SP41 radial tyres standard.
July 1964: Lower-pressure rear brake anti-lock valve fitted.
September 1964: Hydrolastic suspension introduced (Chassis Number C/A2S7 633719 – Austin, and K/A2S4 550743 – Morris). Diaphragm spring clutch introduced (from Engine Number 9FA SA H 3780). Gear-lever now had rubber block insert. New change-speed forks with increased contact area (Engine Number 9FD SA H 1701). Interior gains crushable sun visors and plastic-framed rear-view mirror.
October 1964: New driveshaft coupling for increased torque capacity.
November 1964: Three-position brackets fitted to driver's seat.
January 1965: Improved radiator fitted.
May 1965: Scroll-type oil seal on primary gear.
January 1966: Safety bosses on external door handles (Body Number 47949).
October 1967: Austin and Morris Mini-Cooper MkI discontinued (final Chassis Number 1064385) and replaced by Mini-Cooper MkII.
Total production: Austin 997cc: 12,395; Morris 997cc: 12,465; Total: 24,860. Austin 998cc MkI: 17,737; Morris 998cc MkI: 21,627; Total: 39,364. Total Mini-Cooper MkI: 64,224.

Austin and Morris Mini-Cooper MkII (1967–69)

Coincident with the arrival of the Mini MkII, the Mini-Cooper also received the MkII treatment. The PR slogan earmarked for the MkII Coopers was "The Minis with the Most", with the exhortation: "Take home the world's biggest rally success – and tame it!"

The Mini-Cooper MkII shared most of the bodywork changes of the standard car. These included the new oblong-shaped front grille, larger rear window and bigger rear light clusters. The latter spelled the end of the line for the tubular extensions to the rear overriders which had been a consistent feature of Coopers to date; the front extensions were dispensed with at the same time, although overriders were still fitted at both ends. A new badge on the boot read 'MkII 1000'. Only one trim level was offered, virtually identical to the Mini Super De Luxe specification (see *SECTION FOUR*).

There remained a distinction between the Austin and Morris Mini-Coopers, although at last their radiator grilles were standardized, each with seven thick chrome bars (similar to the type used on the Morris Mini-Cooper MkI). The only distinguishing marks now were the badges with the appropriate Austin or Morris motifs: this was truly the age of badge-engineering. That era ended in 1969 with the arrival of the Mini Clubman. Yet while 'Mini' became the recognized new marque name for the whole range, the Mini-Cooper never had a chance to be so badged: it died at the hands of the new Mini 1275 GT in November 1969.

Specification and performance
As Mini-Cooper MkI, except:
Suspension   Hydrolastic
Weight   1,430lb (650kg)

Optional extras
As Mini-Cooper, except:
Rake-adjustable front seats (from 1969)
Heated rear window (from 1969)

Range
Austin Mini-Cooper MkII (1967–69)
Morris Mini-Cooper MkII (1967–69)

Production history
September 1967: First MkII Cooper produced.
October 1967: Austin and Morris Mini-Cooper MkII introduced (Chassis Number C/AS2B 1068151 – Austin, and Morris – K/A2S6 1069051). Cost: £631.
September 1968: All-synchromesh gearbox introduced (Engine Number 9FX XE H 101).
November 1969: Both Mini-Cooper MkII models discontinued (final Chassis Numbers C/AS2B 1370956 – Austin, and K/A2S6 1365476 – Morris).
Total production: Austin Mini-Cooper MkII: 9,168; Morris Mini-Cooper MkII: 7,228; Total: 16,396.

Austin and Morris Mini-Cooper 'S' 1,071cc (1963–64)

The first Mini-Cooper 'S' was the 1,071cc-engined car, launched prior to the 970cc and 1,275cc versions by virtue of the greater development experience Cooper had had with the A-series

With its 70bhp 1,071cc engine, the 1963 Mini-Cooper 'S' was much more of a performance car than the standard Cooper, with sizzling acceleration for its day. There also came much-needed servo assistance for the front disc brakes. This is a Morris version.

The Mini-Cooper 'S' – of which this is an Austin version – was externally differentiated from the standard Cooper only by its ventilated wheels (here in 3½in form) and small 'S' badges on the bonnet and boot.

engine in the 1,100cc racing category. It was essentially a Mini-Cooper with considerably more performance and larger front disc brakes, a recipe which singularly succeeded.

The powerful, high-revving little engine could be identified by its 11-stud cylinder head with the casting numbers AEG163 or 12G940. Once again there were twin SU HS2 carburettors, but these were fitted with H6 needles.

Externally, the 'S' looked virtually identical to the standard Mini-Cooper, right down to the now-familiar duo-tone paint scheme: indeed, it could only really be identified by its discreet 'S' badges on the bonnet and bootlid, and the standard fitment of ventilated steel wheels, either 3½in or 4½in wide, in both cases minus the standard Cooper's wheeltrims.

Inside, there was special two-tone flecked upholstery and trim to the same standard as the Super De Luxe. The same oval instrument binnacle housed a new speedometer rather optimistically recalibrated to 120mph. A fresh-air heater was standard.

Specification
As Mini-Cooper, except:

Engine	1,071cc four-cylinder OHV
Engine designation	9F/9FD
Bore/stroke	70.64 x 68.26mm
Compression ratio	9:1

Power output	70bhp at 6,200rpm
Torque	62lb.ft at 4,500rpm
Transmission	Four-speed manual: Ratios: 4th 3.765, 3rd 5.1, 2nd 7.21, 1st 12.04; Optional final-drive: 4th 3.44, 3rd 4.66, 2nd 6.59, 1st 11.00; or Optional four-speed close-ratio gearbox with ratios: 4th 3.765, 3rd 4.67, 2nd 6.7, 1st 9.66; Optional final drive: 4th 3.44, 3rd 4.27, 2nd 6.13, 1st 8.84
Brakes	Disc/drum, servo-assisted
Front track	48.4in (1,229mm)
Rear track	46.9in (1,191mm)
Weight	1,410lb (640kg)
Wheels	10 x 3.5in or 10 x 4.5in pressed steel
Tyres	Dunlop 145-10 SP (5.00L-10 option)

Performance

Maximum speed	91mph (146km/h)
0–50mph	9.6sec
0–60mph	13.5sec
30–50mph	10.9sec
40–60mph	11.5sec
50–70mph	14.8sec
Average fuel consumption	29mpg

Optional extras

As Mini-Cooper, except:
Additional 5.5-gallon fuel tank
Oil cooler
Sump guard
5.00L-10 tubed tyres
4½in rims
Straight-cut gears
Factory-manufactured competition parts

NB: Heated rear window and reclining seats not available

Range

Austin Mini-Cooper 'S' (1963–64)
Morris Mini-Cooper 'S' (1963–64)

Production history

March 1963: Austin and Morris Mini-Cooper 'S' launched with 1,071cc engine (Chassis Number C/A2S7 384101 – Austin, and K/A2S4 384601 – Morris). Cost: £695.
August 1963: Improved brake shoes fitted (Chassis Number C/A2S7 384433 – Austin, and K/A2S4 384909 – Morris).
April 1964: Coil-spring clutch replaced by diaphragm clutch.
August 1964: Production of 1071S ceased (final Chassis Number C/A2S7 563570 – Austin, and K/A2S4 563500 – Morris. (final Engine Number 9FD SA H 33948).
Total production: Austin Mini-Cooper 'S' 1,071cc: 2,135; Morris Mini-Cooper 'S' 1,071cc: 1,896. Total: 4,031.

Austin and Morris Mini-Cooper 'S' 970cc (1964–65)

The short-stroke-engined version of the Mini-Cooper 'S' was really nothing more than a homologation special. The 970cc engine was expensive to make, therefore BMC kept it as a special order-only model intended more for competition-minded than for roadgoing drivers. The 970S was the least powerful and slowest of the Mini-Cooper 'S' models, but that belied its sweet and free-revving nature, which allowed it to run surprisingly closely to its sibling models.

In almost all respects it mirrored the specification of the 1071S, with identical brakes, gearbox, wheels, external appearance and interior trim. BMC referred to this model as the Mini-Cooper 'S' 1000, but for convenience it is generally known as the 970S.

The major development for the 970S was the adoption of Hydrolastic suspension only three months into its production life, making the dry rubber cone-suspended 970S a rather rare model. Yet in truth, any 970S was a rare sight as the total production life of the model did not exceed 10 months.

Specification

As Mini-Cooper 'S' 1071, except:
Engine   970cc four-cylinder OHV
Engine designation 9F
Bore/stroke   70.6 x 61.91mm
Compression ratio   10:1
Power output   65bhp at 6,500rpm
Torque   57lb.ft at 5,000rpm
Suspension   Hydrolastic from September 1964

Performance

Maximum speed   89mph (143km/h)
0–50mph   –
0–60mph   11.8sec
30–50mph   –
40–60mph   –
50–70mph   –
Average fuel consumption   30mpg

Range

Austin Mini-Cooper 'S' 1000 (1964–65)
Morris Mini-Cooper 'S' 1000 (1964–65)

Production history

June 1964: Austin and Morris Mini-Cooper 'S' 1000 introduced (Chassis Number C/A2S7 549501 – Austin, and K/A2S4 550501 – Morris. First Engine Number 9F SA X 29001). Cost: £693.
September 1964: Hydrolastic suspension fitted (Chassis Number C/A2S7 549763 – Austin, and K/A2S4 550793 – Morris). Gear-lever in rubber block insert. Crushable sun visor and plastic-framed interior mirror (Body Number 31484).
November 1964: Three-position seat brackets fitted to driver's seat.
April 1965: 970cc-engined Mini-Cooper 'S' discontinued (final Chassis Number C/A2S7 549992 – Austin, and K/A2S4 550980 – Morris).
Total production: Austin Mini-Cooper 'S' 1000: 481; Morris Mini-Cooper 'S' 1000: 482. Total: 963.

Austin and Morris Mini-Cooper 'S' 1275 MkI (1964–67)

BMC's long-stroke development of the Cooper-type A-series engine proved to be the longest-lasting of all the Cooper varieties. The 1,275cc engine with its 81.33mm stroke offered extra power and considerably more torque than the 1,071cc engine it officially replaced.

There was very little to distinguish an early 1275S from the 1071S and 970S. Duo-tone paint schemes were standard, but eventually single-colour schemes were phased in, making the 'S' look more like standard Minis. The ventilated steel wheels remained, and by late 1965 wider 4½in rims were a standard fitment, although the 3½in rims were still an option until the arrival of the MkII.

Inside, the 1275S was again very similar to the earlier 'S' models except that its speedometer was calibrated to no less than 130mph – more than 30mph in excess of the car's capability in standard form.

Like other Minis, the 1275S received Hydrolastic suspension from 1964. Yet the 1275S also gained several unique improvements during its production life: it acquired an oil cooler and twin fuel tanks as standard from 1966 and

received uprated Hydrolastic suspension in the same year. Further, alongside the standard Mini-Cooper, it was the first Mini to be offered with an optional laminated windscreen and reclining front seats. The 1275S moved on to a MkII version in 1967 – see below.

Specification
As Mini-Cooper 'S' 1071, except:

Engine	1,275cc four-cylinder OHV
Engine designation	12F
Bore/stroke	70.6 x 81.33mm
Compression ratio	9.75:1
Power output	76bhp at 5,800rpm
Torque	79lb.ft at 3,000rpm
Suspension	Hydrolastic from September 1964
Front track	47.53in (1,207mm)
Rear track	46.31in (1,176mm)
Weight	1,535lb (698kg)
Fuel tank	Twin 5.5gal tanks = 11gal (50l) from 1966
Luggage capacity	5.5cu ft (0.15cu m) Approx 4cu ft (0.11cu m) from 1966

Performance

Maximum speed	96mph (154km/h)
0–50mph	8.2sec
0–60mph	11.2sec
30–50mph	7.5sec
40–60mph	8.3sec
50–70mph	9.4sec
Average fuel consumption	29mpg

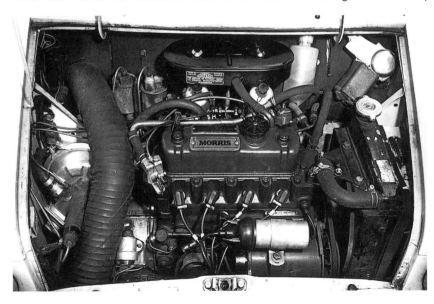

The Cooper 'S' engine can easily be identified by its extra stud and bolt at either end of the cylinder head. This 1,275cc engine delivered a healthy 76bhp.

The most meagre 'S' badge on the bonnet told the world that what you were driving was something special.

Optional extras
As Mini-Cooper 'S' 1071, except:
Laminated windscreen
Reclining front seats (from 1965)
Twin fuel tanks (standard from 1966)
Heated rear window (from 1966)

Range
Austin Mini-Cooper 'S' 1275 MkI (1964–67)
Morris Mini-Cooper 'S' 1275 MkI (1964–67)

Production history
February 1964: First 1275 'S' engine produced (Engine Number 9F SA Y31001).
April 1964: Austin and Morris Mini-Cooper 'S' 1275 introduced (Chassis Number C/A2S7 551501 – Austin, and K/A2S4 552501 – Morris). Cost: £778.
September 1964: Hydrolastic suspension introduced (Chassis Number C/A2S7 552243 – Austin, and K/A2S4 553170 – Morris). Gear-lever gained rubber block insert. Crushable sun visor and plastic-framed interior mirror standard.
November 1964: Three-position seat brackets fitted to driver's seat.
April 1965: Rubber scroll-type oil seal for primary gear.
January 1966: Twin fuel tanks and oil cooler standard (Body Number 47681). Improved camshaft (Engine Number 9F SA Y40006). Safety bosses fitted on external door handles (Body Number 47949).
April 1966: Suspension improvements: higher-rate Hydrolastic units, steel/rubber lower wishbone bush, flange to fix solid UJ on to driveshaft, taper-roller rear hub bearings, extra strengthening for suspension mountings (Chassis Number C/A2S7 851199 – Austin, and K/A2S4 851028 – Morris).
October 1967: Mini-Cooper 'S' MkI replaced by MkII (final Chassis Number C/A2S7 1066319 – Austin, and K/A2S4 1066320 – Morris).
Total production: Austin Mini-Cooper 'S' 1275 MkI: 6,489; Morris Mini-Cooper 'S' 1275 MkI: 7,824. Total: 14,313.

Twin fuel tanks became standard on the 'S' from 1966, as evidenced by the second fuel filler on the offside rear flank.

The Mini-Cooper 'S' received the same MkII treatment as all Minis. The bumper overriders no longer had any tubular extensions. This Austin version is fitted with optional 4½in steel wheels. All MkII wheels had a neutral paint finish instead of white as before.

Austin and Morris Mini-Cooper 'S' MkII (1967–70)

When all other Minis were treated to the MkII bodyshell, the Mini-Cooper 'S' was no exception. It shared the same new oblong radiator grille, enlarged rear window and larger, squarer rear lights as all the other MkII Minis. There was a new 'MkII 1275' badge on the bootlid and a new badge for the bonnet.

As ever, there remained Austin and Morris versions with slightly differing grilles and badges (as per the Mini-Cooper MkII). To distinguish the 'S' from the ordinary Cooper, there were still discreet 'S' badges front and rear, plus wide 4½in rims as standard.

Interestingly, the Mini-Cooper 'S' MkII was the last Mini to be badged Austin and Morris. While all other Minis dropped their marque tags in favour of the new marque name 'Mini' in October 1969, the specialist Austin and Morris Mini-Cooper 'S' models lasted until March 1970 before being replaced by the new Mini-Cooper 'S' MkIII – although the MkIII version had been announced in November 1969, it did not

Unlike the MkI, the seat upholstery of the Cooper 'S' MkII was identical to the Mini Super De Luxe. The speedometer was now calibrated to a wild 130mph. Note the padded dash top rail, common to all MkII Minis, and the control for the optional heated rear window to the left of the switch panel.

The MkII Cooper 'S' bonnet badge.

The Morris bonnet badge had a white background.

actually enter production until early the following year.

Specification
As Mini-Cooper 'S' 1275 MkI, except:
Fuel tank   Two 5.5gal tanks = 11 gal (50l)
Luggage capacity   Approx 4cu ft (0.11cu m)

Optional extras
Reclining front seats (until 1969)
Rake-adjustable front seats (from 1969)
Heated rear window
Sump guard
3.939:1 final drive

Range
Austin Mini-Cooper 'S' MkII (1967–70)
Morris Mini-Cooper 'S' MkII (1967–70)

Production history
October 1967: Austin and Morris Mini-Cooper 'S' MkII introduced (Chassis Number C/A2SB 1068451 – Austin, and K/A2S6 1068471 – Morris). Cost: £849.
October 1968: All-synchromesh gearbox fitted gradually through 1968, with 100 per cent fit from October.
March 1970: MkII discontinued in favour of MkIII (final Chassis Number C/A2SB 1375331 – Austin, and K/A2S6 1375346 – Morris).
Total production: Austin Mini-Cooper 'S' MkII: 2,687; Morris: 3,642. Total: 6,329.

Mini-Cooper 'S' MkIII (1970–71)

This was the final fling for the Mini-Cooper, following the demise of the standard Cooper in 1969. The 'S' was the only Mini-Cooper model to survive the bodywork changes wrought on the whole Mini range in late 1969.

Yet it took a few months for the Mini-Cooper MkIII to enter production with the new-style doors with concealed hinges and wind-up windows, complete with doortrims and seats taken from the Mini Clubman.

It retained the old-style Mini oval instrument nacelle, but for the first time incorporated the same grille as the rest of the Mini range. On the boot was the simple badge 'Mini-Cooper S'. Duo-tone paint finishes were never offered on the Cooper 'S' MkIII.

While most of the rest of the Mini range reverted to the pre-1964 dry rubber-cone system, the Mini-Cooper 'S' soldiered on with Hydrolastic, although some of the very late models may have been fitted with rubber suspension: it seems that BL's Special Tuning department at Abingdon may have been responsible for building up a few more MkIII Cooper 'S' cars after the model was officially withdrawn from production in 1971.

The new bootlid badge common to both Austin and Morris Cooper 'S' MkII models.

From 1970, the Cooper was called just Mini-Cooper 'S'. It incorporated all the MkIII Mini bodyshell changes – including the standard Mini grille instead of a special Cooper one – although bumper over-riders were still standard. *(BMIHT)*

Specification

As Mini-Cooper 'S' MkII, except:

Suspension	Hydrolastic, possibly some dry rubber-cone
Weight	1,525lb (692kg)

Optional extras

Rake-adjustable front seats
Heated rear window
Face-level ventilation

Range

Mini-Cooper 'S' MkIII (1970–71)

Production history

November 1969: Mini-Cooper 'S' MkIII announced.

March 1970: MkIII entered production (Chassis Number XAD1 34127). Flush-fitting doors fitted, along with improved interior trim from Mini Clubman. Cost: £942.

October 1970: Ignition shield fitted. Steering column lock standard on home market.

June 1971: Mini-Cooper 'S' MkIII discontinued (final Chassis Number XAD1 458987).

Total production: 19,511 (of which approx 1,570 cars fully built at Longbridge and approx 18,000 sent as CKD units for foreign assembly).

New bootlid badging for the MkIII brought it into line with the rest of the Mini range.

The major difference in the MkIII 1,275cc 'S' engine was its black, instead of green, paint finish. This unit has non-standard air filters.

The Mini from 1969 to date

In the late Sixties, the British Motor Corporation metamorphosed in a tumult of conglomeration, reorganization and name-changing. When BMC merged with Jaguar, it became British Motor Holdings and then, in 1968, BMH merged again to become the British Leyland Motor Corporation. In its wake, the era of badge-engineering was brought to a studied end. No more strongly was this evidenced than in the Mini range.

From late 1969, Austin and Morris ceased to be used as the marque names for the Mini. The Riley Elf, Wolseley Hornet and Mini Moke had already died. In place of these venerable industry names, the Mini received a dose of British Leyland-style rationalization: all models would now be known simply as 'Mini'. Austin and Morris badges were traded in for British Leyland ones and a new Mini badge appeared on the bonnet. The Mini was the only model in BLMC's range to which this happened, as it had a strong identity of its own.

The policy seemed to work, as the years from 1969 to 1974 were the best in the Mini's history as far as sales were concerned. As the corporate giant was to discover much later, a proliferation of marques was not good for sales in an era when British cars were being attacked by a host of new foreign marques with strong identities. Of course, BL would eventually be rationalized again under the Austin Rover banner, then just Rover, selling all its cars under one name.

From October 1969, all Mini saloons, estates, vans and pick-ups became Minis, under the project codename ADO20. There was much more than just a change of name: the Mini also adopted some long-awaited changes with the so-called Mini MkIII. The bodyshell looked virtually identical to the MkII, but this belied the fact that the whole bodyshell had been almost completely rejigged. One obvious advance was the fitment of enclosed door hinges which finally replaced those symbols of the Mini's cost-cutting origins, external hinges. Other sheet-metal changes included a revised floorpan, boot floor, windscreen surround, front parcel shelf and bonnet hinges.

The doors were also now a little larger and contained the wind-up window mechanism of the defunct Riley Elf/Wolseley Hornet. That meant a reduction in overall elbow width of 5 inches and the end of the carry-all door pockets, a move lamented by many – but such was the price which had to be paid for winding windows. The MkIII bodyshell also marked the end of the drop-down rear number-plate: this was now bolted to a deeper indentation.

More momentous was the decision to return the Mini to the dry rubber-cone suspension fitted on the original-series Minis from 1959 to 1964. This was basically a cost-cutting exercise as the Hydrolastic suspension was considerably more expensive to make, for not much better road performance. Other mechanical improvements introduced across the range were negative-earth electrics and a mechanical fuel pump.

A brand-new top-of-the-range Mini – the Mini Clubman – also arrived in October 1969. This was an entirely marketing-inspired derivative, born of a board-level desire to charge more money for the Mini. The original intention had been to design a new shell with extended front and rear sections, and ex-Ford designer Roy Haynes was called upon to submit proposals. In the event only his front end was used in the new Mini Clubman.

The new nose was far squarer in appearance, with a new grille, lights and bonnet and a higher front bumper. Its effect was to make the Mini some 4 inches longer while incidentally detracting from its appearance. Just about the only point to be said in the Clubman's favour was that it had better under-bonnet access and, perhaps, slightly better accident protection. There was now a lot of space where the radiator would normally be on any other car, but there was nothing to put there – and nothing ever arrived to fill the void.

Further objections to the Mini Clubman were that it was heavier and less aerodynamic, therefore less economical. Being longer, it was also more difficult to park. In short, it was the antithesis of Issigonis' ideals, and he was rightly disgusted by it.

Amazingly, and to the buying public's demerit, the Mini Clubman actually sold very well, nearly half-a-million eventually being purchased. People were basically attracted to the idea of a 'superior' Mini and were happy to pay the extra £45 for the Clubman saloon.

Perhaps they were seduced by the Clubman's

The MkIII Mini bodyshell represented a major sheet metal revision of the Mini. Although it looked little different – the only major external changes were the lack of door hinges and new winding windows – the new body in fact incorporated larger door apertures, a revised floorpan, new boot floor and lid, windscreen, front parcel shelf and bonnet hinge spacing. This is an Austrian-spec model with different front indicators.

more modern interior. It had the same level of trim as the Super De Luxe, but came with new doortrims and a squarish twin-dial instrument nacelle sited, for the first time in a Mini, ahead of the driver. There was also face-level ventilation.

The Mini Clubman was initially only available with the 998cc engine, but in saloon form it retained the Hydrolastic suspension abandoned by all other Minis bar the Cooper 'S'. The Clubman was finally converted to dry cone suspension in June 1971.

Based on the Clubman saloon bodyshell was BLMC's new Cooper successor, the Mini 1275 GT. This might have been a better car than the Mini-Cooper (indeed, BLMC's marketing line was: "Carries on where the Cooper left off"), but most opinion confirms that it was a step backwards. The real problem was the engine. The 1,275cc unit was not at all the same as that used by the Mini-Cooper 'S', being taken instead from the Austin/Morris 1300. This was a logical and, above all, cost-effective way to yield a fast Mini. The engine was manufactured without the Cooper's emphasis on a performance specification: both its head and block were different from that of the 1275S, and it only had a single carburettor. It gave a mere 59bhp (17bhp less than the Cooper 'S'), although it had more torque. Ultimately, it provided inferior performance.

To try to compensate, BL fitted the 1275 GT with a lower final-drive ratio (3.65:1 from 3.44:1), which gave the car a top speed of 87mph, but

it returned such poor fuel consumption that it reverted to the 3.44:1 ratio the following year, albeit with the closer lower gear ratios of the original gearbox. Yet it was never a car with the same verve or charisma as the Mini-Cooper. In its favour, it was certainly cheaper.

Like the Clubman saloon, the 1275 GT had Hydrolastic suspension until 1971, then dry rubber-cone suspension. It also had Cooper 'S' disc front brakes. Unlike any other Mini before, it was also fitted with a rev-counter, something the faster and more overtly sporting Mini-Cooper had never received.

The final Mini Clubman variant was the estate. In fact, this was the only post-1969 Mini estate offered, as the standard-bodyshell estates died with the relaunch of the Mini as a marque in itself. The Clubman estate mirrored the specification of the Clubman saloon, but was never available with wooden battens like the earlier estate: instead, there was a strip of mock wood trim down each flank. It was the only 1969 Mini Clubman variety to retain dry suspension.

The Mini 850, 1000 and Clubman were all initially available with automatic transmission: only the 1275 GT was not. The 850 automatic died within two years, leaving the 1000 as the standard automatic model. The later Mini Clubman 1100 models were never sold with automatic transmission: if an automatic Clubman was wanted after 1975, it had to be ordered specially and would be supplied with the 998cc engine.

In summary, the Mini range for most of the Seventies consisted of five basic models: 850, 1000, Clubman saloon, Clubman estate and 1275 GT. The publicity hype told buyers that the new Mini was "your kind of car" and, more improbably, that the Mini was "the only truly sensible car to drive today". The public lapped them up and the Mini clocked up its most successful ever years: almost 1.5 million were made between 1970 and 1974, the all-time best year being 1971, when 318,475 Minis were made worldwide, making it easily BL's most successful car. In 1973, BL was able to boast that there were more Minis on British roads than any other car, the Mini being one of the few cars whose sales actually benefited from the OPEC oil crisis of the early Seventies, especially the 850 model.

During the Seventies, BL needed to make very few changes to the extremely popular Mini range, which was just as well because it had very little spare cash around to do so. The major change of the first half of the decade was a new gearbox with a rod-operated change. Seat belts and a heater were at last made a standard feature on the basic 850 in 1974, although for some time previously a 850 could not be bought without these items fitted, hence they were 'compulsory options' for which BL always charged extra!

Another familiar member of the A-series engine family, the 1,098cc unit fitted to the Morris 1100 from as early as 1962, finally made it into a Mini from 1975 with the Mini Clubman 1100. This unit was simply a 998cc engine stroked to 83.8mm, and was then currently in use in the base-model Allegro. The engine was also used in the standard Mini bodyshell from 1977, but was for export markets only. The same was true of the Mini 1300. For details of both these models, see *SECTION NINE: International Minis*. For a time during the Seventies, and particularly during the strike-torn years at BL, many Minis were imported from BL's Belgian plant at Seneffe, where they were built in large numbers.

Minis grew gradually more refined through the Seventies, with better equipment and trim. However, they hardly changed at all in appearance, although the 1275 GT became the first Mini to wear 12in wheels from 1974 and was the first small car to be offered with Denovo run-flat tyres, also in 1974. The Denovo tyres were designed so that in the event of a puncture a journey could be continued without having to change the wheel, by virtue of a rubber-based rim fitted to the edge of the wheel. The design

succeeded, but there was some question over the ride and handling with Denovos fitted. Some asked if it was worth suffering an inferior ride for the sake of not having to change a wheel in the rare instance of getting a puncture.

Matt-black grilles became standard in 1977, but apart from that, there was very little to distinguish a 1979 from a 1970 Mini. In 1978, sales ducked under 200,000 for the first time since 1961, and it began to look as though the sun might finally be setting on the Mini.

By then, plans had already been afoot for two years for a Mini replacement, codenamed ADO88. This would have been a three-door hatchback only 6 inches longer than the Mini, styled by Harris Mann. It reached full-scale model size, but the project was redirected under BL's new Chairman, Michael Edwardes, and became the larger LC8 project – which would in turn evolve into the Austin Mini Metro. This arrived in 1980 and, although it caused an immediate halving of Mini sales, it was never meant as, or ever became, a replacement for the Mini – at least, not the standard Mini saloon.

The Mini Clubman and 1275 GT were phased out as anachronisms when the Metro arrived and few mourned their loss. The Mini estate – now no longer badged as a Clubman – which had been BL's solitary, and rather embarrassing, competitor in the growing class of 'superminis' like Ford's Fiesta, continued to be sold until stocks were exhausted in 1982.

By 1976, Leyland Cars and its predecessors had produced 4 million Minis worldwide. The then Miss Britain, Sue Cuff, sits in an already out-of-fashion mini-skirt on an in-fashion Mini 1275 GT. The Mini outnumbered all other cars on British roads throughout the Seventies, when it chalked up its most successful years in sales terms.

The historic 5 millionth Mini rolled off the Longbridge production line at 12.30pm on February 19, 1986. This massive figure makes it easily the best-selling British car, and it is a record which will never be broken by a British manufacturer.

Another casualty in 1980 was the Mini 850. After 22 years in production, the 848cc-engined saloon was judged to be too slow to be competitive. As such, there really remained just one model: the Mini 1000, which was offered in two trim levels, City and HL. The 998cc engine was in fact a new version of the A-series unit, developed for the Metro and known as the A-plus. It had a stiffer block, tougher exhaust valves, a crankshaft torsional damper, hydraulic timing-chain tensioner, spade-type oil pump and a more durable crankshaft. With its single HS4 SU carburettor, revised manifolding, twin exhaust outlets, revised camshaft, advanced timing and increased valve lift, its output increased to 39bhp, an extra 1bhp.

The transmission was revised, too: the gears were given larger needle roller bearings and tighter tolerances. Combined with better standards of build quality, BL gave the revised cars the title of 'Quiet Mini', reflecting their increased refinement. Interiors were improved with new seat fabrics and a steering wheel from the Metro.

In the Eighties, the Mini remained unique.

There was nothing else like it: it occupied a size and class of its own. Even the tiny Fiat 126 was slightly longer than the Mini, while having a more cramped interior, dismal performance and zero refinement. The Mini was still cheap to buy entering the Eighties and, more importantly for the manufacturer, was still cheap to make. Indeed, it became cheaper as, from 1980, the final stages of assembly took place in the same production facility as the Metro, which reduced costs.

Fuel economy became the central issue for the Mini in 1982 as the range was revised in the form of the City E and 1000 HLE. Both had a high-compression head and a 2.95:1 final-drive ratio, which made them exceptionally economical at touring speeds. The HLE was quickly replaced by the Mini Mayfair, a name which was then appearing on several other BL products like the Metro. This was getting to be quite a sophisticated – even indulgent – little car compared with previous Minis.

An important further rationalization took place in 1984 with the standardization of 12in wheels and front disc brakes across the Mini range. At the same time, the rear drum brakes were uprated, along with the tyres.

A surprise for everyone was how resilient the Mini remained through the Eighties. Sales consistently exceeded targets and many export markets actually grew. Marketing men were dumbfounded when it turned out that the higher-spec Mini Mayfair was selling better than the basic model by a ratio of 60:40. They thought – wrongly – that, as a result of the Metro, buyers would opt for the cheaper version. Times were changing, though, and the economy appeal which had been the foundation of the first Minis was fast disappearing.

The success of the 'luxury' Mayfair may partially explain the rash of special-edition Minis which exploded during the Eighties. Buyers responded well to each new limited-edition model until they became an annual Austin Rover exercise. The first British-market special edition Mini had arrived in 1976 with the Limited Edition Mini 1000, complete with orange-striped trim and green-and-white paintwork. Many others followed. See *SECTION FIVE* for the complete story of all the Mini special editions.

Perversely, during Harold Musgrove's years at the helm of BL, Austin badges reappeared on Mini grilles during the mid-Eighties. Given that the Mini had become a well-established marque for over 10 years, this was a mystifying move.

The badges were not removed until 1987, when Austin effectively ceased as a marque and not one model in Austin Rover's range was ever again so badged.

Following the switch to 12in wheels and disc front brakes in 1984, a series of changes moved the Mini gently upmarket. The familiar circular central instrument pod – first seen on the very first Mini and still fitted to the City E until 1985 – finally gave way to a more conventional binnacle sited in the line of the driver's sight. Interiors became much more luxurious than any Mini previously, with velour in the Mayfair and colour co-ordination the order of the day.

Yet Minis were really given comparatively little development during the Eighties. There was simply no need, as around 40,000 a year were regularly sold throughout the decade. Strong demand from France, Germany and especially Japan kept the Mini's chances of staying in production well and truly alive – despite the persistent rumours, well-founded in retrospect, that the Mini might be due for the chop.

1986 saw Mini production pass the 5 million mark. It is easily the best-selling British car ever made, and just about scrapes into the chart for the all-time top 10 best-selling cars worldwide. Ironically, in the mid-Eighties Austin Rover was seriously considering axing the Mini, but when the news leaked out, it received a flood of letters imploring it not to end production; since then, the Mini has never been short of development.

Rover claimed that the Mini was the first small car in Britain to become available with a catalytic converter, which was introduced as a dealer-fitted option in 1989, no engine modifications being required. A catalyst did not become a standard Mini fitment until the 1.3-litre engine was standardized across the range in 1992.

With the Mini Racing and Flame special editions of 1989, Rover was getting fairly close to reproducing the look of a Mini-Cooper: duo-tone paint schemes, alloy wheels and so on. It came even closer by offering, with official endorsement, a John Cooper Conversion Kit as an optional extra from 1989. This included twin SU HS2 carburettors, a polished flowed cylinder head and uprated exhaust system. This boosted power by 19bhp to 59bhp at 6,000rpm, with torque rising to 64lb.ft at 3,500rpm. That made quite a difference to the 998cc engine – and was popular enough for Rover to raise its corporate eyebrow.

Few people could have imagined that Rover would revive a model which had been defunct for nearly 20 years, but Rover did just that with the brand-new Mini-Cooper of 1990. The new version was a very different animal from the one last bearing the Cooper name, which had gone out of production in 1971. John Cooper had been modifying Minis himself since the mid-Eighties and calling them Mini-Coopers, then Rover stepped in. It bought the rights to the Cooper name from the TKM Group – which by then owned the Cooper Car Company – and proceeded to make its own official Mini-Coopers, complete with John Cooper's signature on the bonnet. The difference was, John Cooper had no royalties this time round.

The 1990 Mini-Cooper was basically an adaptation of the Mini Thirty special edition bodyshell with a 61bhp single-carburettor catalyst version of the 1,275cc A-series engine recently used in the – now dead – MG Metro. Thus it was not the great Mini-Cooper 'S' successor that it might have been, but was undoubtedly still the best production Mini of modern times: it would do 92mph and accelerate from 0–60mph in 12.2sec. From 1991, however, a Performance Conversion Kit

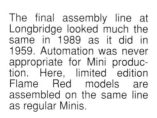

The final assembly line at Longbridge looked much the same in 1989 as it did in 1959. Automation was never appropriate for Mini production. Here, limited edition Flame Red models are assembled on the same line as regular Minis.

could be bought for the Cooper through Rover dealers or John Cooper Garages, which effectively produced a modern version of the Mini-Cooper 'S'. Its performance at last matched the old 1275 Cooper 'S': nearly 100mph top speed and 0–60mph in around 10sec.

The Cooper was also the most luxurious Mini yet produced by the factory in its original limited edition, having such extravagances as leather trim, a red steering wheel, wooden dashboard and tinted glass. The first 1,000 UK-market cars had white stripes down the bonnet upon which was inscribed a 'John Cooper' signature; thereafter, they were rather less well equipped and had plain bonnets.

The main change to the Mini-Cooper was the fitment of fuel injection from 1991, which gave an extra 2bhp. This in turn meant that in-gear acceleration was marginally improved. Apart from a slight increase in noise levels, the improvement was generally welcomed. The Cooper became an important model in the Mini range, accounting for 40 per cent of Mini sales worldwide.

The Mini City, which had remained the identity of the base Mini since 1979, was replaced by a new model, the Mini Sprite, from 1992. This event marked the end of the 1-litre-engined Longbridge Minis after no less than 31 years in production. The Sprite and Mayfair now had the 1.3-litre catalyst-equipped carburettor engine with 50bhp on tap. Yet the 998cc powertrain did not die. Rover continued making it for export to Portugal – for the Moke – and to Venezuela (for the glassfibre-bodied MiniCord).

The final evolution of the Mini at the time of writing is the Cabriolet, an idea tried by many specialists over the years, notably Crayford in the Sixties. The first type that could have been bought from Rover dealers was an officially approved conversion effected by a German Rover dealer in 1991.

Yet the 'official' Mini Cabriolet was first seen at the Birmingham Motor Show in 1992, although it did not actually make it into production until July the following year. Its hood was manually-operated and was of the 'pram' variety, with a very high profile when folded back; many thought it very ugly. It had the same fuel-injected 1.3-litre engine as the Mini-Cooper (indeed, it was sold in some foreign markets as the Mini-Cooper i Cabriolet). No other Mini was so luxuriously appointed as this: Revolution alloy wheels with locking nuts, burr-walnut veneer dashboard and cappings, even a standard clock! However, such luxuries certainly came at a price: no less than £11,995, compared with only £6,995 for the Mini-Cooper. Nevertheless, at a production rate of 15 per week, the Cabriolet never suffered from a shortage of buyers.

The Mini range in 1994 consisted of four models: the Sprite, Mayfair, Cooper and Cabriolet, all with the same-capacity 1,275cc engine, but in two forms: carburettor and injection. It was a tremendously popular range, still the best-selling Rover model in many export markets, especially Japan, where at one stage the Mini accounted for 98 per cent of Rover sales! Japan remained the largest market for the Mini anywhere in the world, with 8,681 sales in 1993, compared with UK sales of 6,326.

Even the entry-level Sprite was better-equipped than the best-trimmed models of the Sixties, and a very far cry from the spartan Mini as launched in 1959, with fitments like disc front brakes, a catalyzed engine, smart trim and modern security equipment.

Yet so much remained the same. The shape was virtually unaltered, right down to the external seams, cheeky nose, drop-down boot and the choice of fixed or hinged rear quarter-windows. The same rubber suspension sat under the body, there were still, of course, the same subframes carrying all the mechanicals, and even the engine was still from the same old A-series stable.

It still received accolades. In 1991, *Autocar & Motor* voted the Mini "the greatest car of all time" and the same year *What Car?* said the Cooper was their Alternative Car of the Year. *Car* magazine voted it as one of its top 10 favourite cars, adding in September 1994 that it "makes every other car seem flat and flabby".

The latest Mini may be a gracefully pampered old lady, but its heart remains pure Mini. The question remains: for how much longer? Its qualities of simplicity, economy and size remain as pertinent today as they were in 1959 – if not more so. People all over the world still want Minis. The most dangerous threats to its survival are politics and safety legislation.

In January 1994, BMW announced that it was taking control of the Rover Group. Ironically, Issigonis and Bernd Pieschetsrieder (the Chairman of BMW who orchestrated the takeover) were distantly related. There were conflicting reports about whether BMW would keep the Mini going, but it seemed unlikely that it would pull the plug on such a popular model.

The severest test of the Mini's survival power

John Cooper stands beside the new-generation Mini-Cooper at Goodwood. In spirit – if not ultimate performance – it was a successful rekindling of the original Mini-Cooper magic. Inset is a shot of the 1961 Mini-Cooper, also in the pits at Goodwood, and reproduced separately on page 38.

must be future and stricter European crash tests, should they come into force in the late Nineties. Whether the Mini's antiquated body construction would pass such tests without major retooling is very much in doubt. As far as emissions go, the venerable A-series engine is quite capable of coping with all future worldwide tests. Rover's official line is: "The Mini is a valued car in Rover's product portfolio, and Rover envisages it continuing in production for as long as it continues to sell."

By April 1994, the grand total of all Minis produced worldwide was 5,280,865. Incredibly, it remained Britain's best-selling export car. It is hard to argue with the conclusion that the Mini is the best car that Britain has ever produced – and probably the best small car the world has ever seen.

Mini 850 (1969–80) and Mini 850 City (1979–80)

The basic Mini in the range, the 850, continued in MkIII form with a bodyshell that looked almost identical to the MkII except for its concealed door hinges. Common to all Minis from October 1969, it received the Riley Elf-type doors with winding windows. The suspension reverted from Hydro-lastic to the original non-fluid cone system.

The Austin and Morris badges were thrown away for a new Mini motif placed on the bonnet. The badge on the rear end read 'Mini 850' and there were new British Leyland emblems on the front wings, just in front of the doors.

The Mini 850 continued the spirit of the early Minis throughout the Seventies: its fitment of the old 848cc engine, direct gearchange, and its lack of brightwork, wheeltrims, heater and passenger's visor made it basic in the extreme.

Unlike the MkII, there was only one basic 850 model available in Britain (export markets were also offered an 850 Special De-Luxe). This most basic Mini had essentially the same trim as the old standard MkII, with the single-dial instrument nacelle, fixed rear quarter-windows, optional heater and only one sun visor.

While the 1000 models had the remote gearchange of the ex-Mini-Cooper, the 850 had to make do with the old-style direct change, complete with cranked gear-lever, something it did not lose until the end of 1972. Automatic transmission was an option only until 1971; thereafter, it was only available on the 1000 and Clubman.

During the changeover from Austin/Morris to Mini, there was some mixing-up of parts, meaning that sometimes a Mini could be bought with minor items of trim bearing Austin or Morris emblems, but this situation persisted only for a short while.

Seat belts were listed as standard "at extra cost" and fitment of the heater was effectively the same, but from 1974, inertia-reel belts and a heater were included in the list price. In 1976, the 850 received an improved-specification interior with twin stalk controls, larger pedals, a new rocker switch panel with controls for choke, hazard lights, heated rear window, brake circuit failure test, lights and heater control, plus a new ignition lock. In 1977, the 850 looked a little different, with a matt black grille and a revised steering wheel.

The final 850 variant was the short-lived Mini 850 City of 1979. This was a new entry-level

A familiar sight: the crude trim of the Mini 850. This is a post-1976 model with standard heater, rocker switches and remote gearchange. However, owners still had to make do with just one instrument dial containing the speedo, warning lamps and fuel gauge.

Even in 1977 the Mini 850 was selling very well. It received a minor facelift with a matt-black front grille and by this time it had brightwork around the windscreen. Inside, it received a new steering wheel.

model distinguished by its black bumpers, rain gutter and wheelarches and a three-quarter-length coachline with a 'City' logo on each front wing and on the boot. At the same time, a new 850 Super De Luxe was introduced with essentially the same equipment as the 1000: for instance, hinged rear quarter-lights, three-gauge oval dial and better upholstery.

On the introduction of the Mini Metro in 1980, all Mini 850 models were discontinued, although the 848cc engine continued to be available in the Mini van for a further two years.

Specification

Engine	848cc four-cylinder OHV
Engine designation	8MB, 8AH with automatic gearbox
Bore/stroke	62.94 x 68.25mm
Compression ratio	8.3:1 (8.8:1 with automatic gearbox)
Power output	33bhp at 5,300rpm
Torque	44lb.ft at 2,900rpm
Transmission	Four-speed all-synchromesh manual: Ratios: 4th 3.765, 3rd 5.395, 2nd 8.35, 1st 13.27, Rev 13.34 Four-speed automatic optional
Steering	Rack-and-pinion
Brakes	Drum/drum
Suspension	Independent front, double wishbones with rubber cones and telescopic dampers. Independent rear, trailing arms with rubber cones and telescopic dampers
Wheels	10 x 3.5in pressed steel
Tyres	10 x 5.20in Dunlop tubeless cross-ply Dunlop 145SR-10in radial-ply (from 1973)
Wheelbase	80.2in (2,036mm)
Length	120.25in (3,054mm)
Width	55.5in (1,410mm)
Height	53in (1,346mm)
Front track	47.8in (1,214mm)
Rear track	46.4in (1,179mm)
Weight	1,360lb (617kg)
Fuel tank	5.5gal (25l) – 7.5gal (34l) from 1980
Luggage capacity	5.5cu ft (0.16cu m) – 4.1cu ft (0.116cu m) from 1980

Performance

Maximum speed	77mph (124km/h)
0–50mph	13.0sec
0–60mph	20.3sec
30–50mph	13.7sec
40–60mph	16.8sec
50–70mph	28.0sec

The 850 City became the new base model in 1979. It now looked much more distinctive, with bold black coachlines and decals. Chrome bumpers gave way to matt black-painted items and there was black trim for the wheel-arches, sills and rain gutters.

Average fuel consumption	38mpg
Government fuel test	
(Urban/56mph/75mph)	39.3/48.7/–

Optional extras
Heater (until 1974)
Passenger's sun visor
Radial-ply tyres (from 1971 to 1973)
Cross-ply tyres (1973 only)
Rake-adjustable front seats (until 1971)
Heated rear window (until 1976)
Automatic transmission (until 1971)
Black paintwork (except City)

Range
Mini 850 (1969–79)
Mini City (1979–80)
Mini 850 Super De Luxe (1979–80)

Production history
August 1969: Production of Mini 850 began (Chassis Number X/A2S1 112).
October 1969: Mini 850 launched. Cost: £596.
December 1970: Some models fitted with a steering lock.
1971: Radiator cowling abandoned.
February 1972: Improved synchromesh (from Engine Number 85H 387E H 109003).
April 1972: Split-type needle roller bearings fitted to idler gears, introduced progressively then 100% fit from Engine Number 85H 387E H 125102.

December 1972: Improved driveshaft boot and longer-life chassis (Chassis Number X/A2S1 799557A). Alternator standard. Rod-operated remote-control gearchange standard.
February 1973: Radial-ply tyres standard.
April 1973: New driveshaft with plunging CV inboard joints.
June 1973: Improved door check pivot brackets fitted.
October 1973: Low-octane fuel distribution discontinued.
February 1974: Inertia-reel seat belts standard.
April 1974: Fresh-air heater standard on all models.
May 1974: SU HS4 swing-needle carburettor and revised manifold, air cleaner and exhaust manifold fitted. Ignition timing altered.
June 1974: Heated rear window standard, and twin-silencer exhaust fitted (new chassis-numbering system: Chassis Number XK2S1 101).
July 1974: Passenger's-side sun visor and door mirror standard.
October 1975: New expanded vinyl seat trim covering new seat frames with anti-tip catches; seat belt anchorages located in rear door pockets instead of floor; front and rear door pocket trim restyled; 88° thermostat standard (Chassis Number XK2S1 259845).
May 1976: Twin column-mounted control stalks fitted, new rocker-switch-type panel incorporating hazard lights standard, larger pedals from Allegro, moulded carpets and ignition/steering

lock from BL Princess fitted and suspension modified with softer rear springs and damper settings, plus new subframe mounts (Chassis Number XK2S1 340101).

July 1977: Matt black grille, vanity mirror standard, with padded steering wheel and handbrake grip from Austin Allegro (Chassis Number XK2S1 453376).

July 1979: Mini 850 replaced by Mini City (Chassis Number XK2S1 633177) and Mini 850 Super De Luxe (Chassis Number XK2S1N 635039). Cost: £2,289 and £2,482 respectively. City without heated rear window and with Houndstooth check cloth upholstery, City decals and black bumpers. Super De Luxe with striped fabric seats, fitted carpets, three-gauge oval nacelle, face-level ventilation, etc as per Mini 1000.

Early 1980: 7.5-gallon fuel tank standard.

May 1980: Extensive sound-deadening material fitted, plus new perforated headlining.

August 1980: Production of Mini City ended (final Chassis Number XK2S1000 743113) and Mini 850 SDL (final Chassis Number XK2S1N00 743003).

September 1980: Models officially withdrawn from sale as 998cc-engined City replaced 848cc City.

Total production: Approx 407,670.

Inside the 850 City there was jazzy new upholstery in the form of Houndstooth cloth seat facings with black PVC borders and seat backs. Cloth trim on the entry-level Mini was definitely something of a novelty.

Mini 1000 (1969–82), Mini City [998cc] (1980–92) and Mini Mayfair [998cc] (1982–92)

The single Mini 1000 model available from October 1969 was basically a continuation of the old MkII 1000 Super De Luxe, with the new ADO20 bodyshell: like all Minis from 1969, the Mini 1000 came with wind-up windows and concealed door hinges. Again, dry rubber suspension became standard.

Inside, the 1000 was distinctly superior to the 850, corresponding to the old Super De Luxe specification. Hence it had the oval three-instrument nacelle, a standard heater, two sun visors, better trim and hinged rear-quarter windows. Externally, it could be distinguished by bright-work around the windscreen, wheel rim embellishers and its rear badge.

The 1000 received most of the improvements to the 850 model including radial-ply tyres, better springing, the new rod change-type gearbox, improved synchromesh, standard alternator, inertia-reel seat belts and heated rear window. It also eventually acquired reclining seats and reversing lights.

When the 850 Super De Luxe was introduced in 1979, the 1000 was confusingly renamed the 1000 Super. When the 850 models died in 1980, a new model simply called City was launched, which was basically the same as the 850 City, but with the 998cc engine. There was little to distinguish it externally from the 850cc City apart from the 1981 model year new-style motif in the centre of the grille and a new Mini logo on the bonnet, which became standardized across the Mini range in October 1980.

Coinciding with the launch of the Mini Metro, a number of Metro parts were transferred to the Mini: the 1000 Super was given a big revamp and renamed the 1000 HL, gaining a Clubman interior – complete with double-gauge instrument pod – and the A-plus engine and transmission from the Metro. A Mini 1000 HL estate also appeared in the sales lists, but this was simply a rebadged Mini Clubman estate with the same mechanical and trim changes as the 1000 HL

The City's dashboard was the same as ever, offering no more than was absolutely necessary for travel, complete with the single-dial nacelle. This model has an optional panel to the right for a foglamp switch.

saloon and a 998cc engine.

In 1982, the estate was discontinued because the supply of bodyshells had dried up. Also that year came the economy-conscious City E and 1000 HLE models, with new 2.95:1 final drives and high-compression cylinder heads. The City E continued in production, gradually gaining better trim, colour-keyed trim parts, side-mounted indicators and different colour exterior trim (Nimbus – a sort of grey sheen – instead of black).

In common with all Minis, 12in wheels and front disc brakes became standard from 1984. Face-level ventilation, first offered as a Mini 1000 option in 1969, finally became standard on the City E from 1985, and at the same time the famous central dial gave way to a two-dial instrument pod and the City logo was moved from the doors to the rear quarter-panel. The 'E' tag was dropped in 1988 and the City was finally killed off along with the 998cc engine in 1992.

The 1000 HLE, meanwhile, transmuted in 1982 into the Mini Mayfair, reviving a prewar Austin name. Henceforth the Mayfair became the 'luxury' Mini in the range. It had smart new Raschelle velour upholstery – as seen in the Metro Vanden Plas – cut-pile carpeting, tinted glass, standard radio, head restraints, passenger door mirror and locking fuel filler.

From late 1985, the Mayfair gained a host of interior trim improvements – coinciding with the improved City E – and was immediately distinguishable externally by its new full-width wheel-trims. The single-dial central instrument binnacle of the City finally gave way to a twin binnacle mounted in front of the driver at the same time. The Mayfair was progressively treated to mildly more luxurious equipment, but its life in 1-litre form ended in 1992 when the Rover Group switched from the 998cc engine to the 1,275cc unit. The Mayfair continued with the 1.3-litre A-series engine (see below), while the City gave way to the new 1.3-litre Sprite. Automatic transmission was always available as an option on all versions of the Mini 1000 from 1969 to 1992.

The Mini 850 Super De Luxe lasted for only one year, from 1979 to 1980. It was a more upmarket 850, with the same equipment and trim as the Mini 1000, and was easily distinguishable by its twin coachlines under the windows and hinged rear quarter-windows.

Specification

	1000/City/1000 HL	HLE/City E/Mayfair
As Mini 850, except:		
Engine	998cc four-cylinder OHV	998cc four-cylinder OHV
Engine designation	99H/A+ from 1980	A+
Bore/stroke	64.59 x 76.2mm	64.59 x 76.2mm
Compression ratio	8.3:1	10.3:1
	8.9:1 (auto 'box)	
Power output	38bhp at 5,250rpm	40bhp at 5,000rpm
	39bhp at 4,750rpm (from 1980)	
	41bhp at 4,850rpm (auto 'box)	
Torque	52lb.ft at 2,700rpm	50lb.ft at 2,500rpm
	52lb.ft at 2,000rpm (from 1980)	
Transmission	Four-speed synchromesh manual:	Ratios: 4th 2.95, 3rd 4.23,
	Ratios: 4th 3.44, 3rd 4.93, 2nd	2nd 6.54, 1st 10.43
	7.63, 1st 12.13	
	Optional four-speed automatic	
Brakes	Drum/drum	Disc/drum from 1984
Wheels	3.5 x 10in	3.5 x 10in
	10in x 5J optional (from 1982)	
Tyres	5.20 x 10in	Dunlop LRR 145 SR-10
		165/70 with 10in alloy
		145 SR-12 (from 1984)
Weight	1,375lb (625kg)	1,375lb (625kg)
Fuel tank	5.5gal (25l), 7.5gal (34l) from 1980	
Luggage capacity	5.5cu ft (0.16cu m), 4.1cu ft (0.116cu m) from 1980	

Performance

	1000/City/1000 HL	HLE/City E/Mayfair
Maximum speed	82mph (132km/h)	82mph (132km/h)
0–50mph	12.5sec	11.3sec
0–60mph	18.7sec	17.5sec
30–50mph	12.3sec	14.0sec
40–60mph	15.5sec	15.9sec
50–70mph	23.8sec	23.9sec
Average fuel consumption	35mpg	40mpg
Government fuel test (Urban/56mph/75mph)	38.8/48.5/33.0 (sal)	45.9/60.5/44.1
	37.5/47.7/32.8 (est)	(manual)
	40.2/38.9/– (auto sal)	40.9/46.1/–
	37.4/36.3/– (auto est)	(auto)

With its MkII-style wheeltrims, extra brightwork and opening rear windows, the Mini 1000 was an easily-spotted upmarket Mini. The 998cc engine gave it significantly better mid-range performance.

The 1000 boasted the three-gauge oval nacelle, remote gearchange and superior vinyl upholstery. All Minis from 1969 had winding windows. Face-level ventilation was initially an option, but became standard from 1976.

The Mini's boot space was the same as ever: a small volume accessed by a drop-down tailgate. The Mini from 1969 lost the hinging number-plate, which thenceforth rendered carrying loads with the bootlid down illegal.

In July 1977, the 1000 was given a facelift consisting of a matt black grille, twin coach-lines under the windows, standard reversing lights and the deletion of the bright wheeltrims first seen in 1959.

Inside the post-1977 1000 there were reclining striped cropped nylon seats, front door map pockets and a dipping rear-view mirror.

An X-ray view of the so-called 'Quiet Mini'. Launched in the summer of 1980, it incorporated extensive sound-deadening in the floorpan, front bulkhead, dashboard, roof and boot, plus a new headlining material. The effect was to produce what could be more accurately described as a 'quieter Mini'.

Performance

Maximum speed	84mph (135km/h)
0–60mph	19.7sec
30–50mph	–
40–60mph	–
50–70mph	27.5sec
Average fuel consumption	40mpg
Government fuel test (Urban/56mph/75mph)	46.1/60.5/40.7

Optional extras

Automatic transmission
Bumper overriders (until 1971)
Face-level ventilation (until 1976)
Rake-adjustable seats (until 1977)
Heated rear window (until 1974 – optional for City until 1982)
Radial-ply tyres (until 1973)
Cropped nylon seat facings (from 1975–77)
Black, metallic paint (for all models – except City from 1983 only)
Clearcoat metallic paint
Alloy wheels with wheelarch extensions for Mayfair only (from 1982 to 1984)
12in alloy wheels for Mayfair only (from 1984)
Rear lap seat belts (from 1984–88)
Stereo radio/cassette for Mayfair only (from 1985–88)
Catalytic convertor (from 1989)
John Cooper Performance Kit (from 1989)
  – not available for automatic or catalyst-equipped cars.

Specification   Mayfair/City (from 1988)

As Mini City E, except:

Power output	42bhp at 5,250rpm
Torque	58lb.ft at 2,600rpm
Brakes	Disc/drum
Transmission	Four-speed manual: Ratios: 4th 3.105, 3rd 4.42, 2nd 6.78, 1st 11.32, Rev 11.38 Optional 4-speed automatic: Ratios: 4th 3.27, 3rd 4.77, 2nd 6.03, 1st 8.80, Rev 8.80
Wheels	12in
Tyres	Dunlop 145/70 SR-12
Weight	1,495lb (680kg)
Fuel tank	7.5gal (34l)
Luggage capacity	4.1cu ft (0.116cu m)

The revised and pared-down Mini range from October 1980, consisting of only three models: from left to right, the 1000 HL, 1000 HL Estate and City. The Estate was merely a rebadged Clubman Estate and the City now had the 1-litre engine. Note the new Mini badge on the bonnet and the Austin Morris Group badge in the centre of the grille. The Estate had also lost the vertical bar from its grille.

Range

Mini 1000 (1969–79)
Mini 1000 Super (1979–80)
Mini City (1980–82/1988–92)
Mini City E (1982–88)
Mini 1000 HL (1980–82)
Mini 1000 HL Estate (1980–82)
Mini 1000 HLE (1982)
Mini Mayfair (1982–92)

Production history

As Mini 850, except:
September 1969: Production of Mini 1000 began (Chassis Number X/A2S1-N 601).
October 1969: Mini 1000 launched. Cost: £675.
January 1971: Some models fitted with steering lock.
February 1972: Improved synchromesh from engine 99H 353EH 275337.
April 1972: Split needle-roller bearings on idler gear from engine 99H 353EH 309615.
June 1974: As 850 but better carpets with stronger backing fitted. New chassis numbering from Chassis Number XL2S1N 101.
May 1976: Face-level ventilation standard (Chassis Number XL2S1N 340554).
July 1977: Two-tone striped cropped nylon trim, rake-adjustable seats, front door map pockets, dipping rear-view mirror and reversing lights standard. Coachlines added below windows.

October 1979: Mini 1000 redesignated Mini 1000 Super with painted coachline (Chassis Number XL2S1N 633285). Cost: £2,829.
September 1980: Mini City introduced with 998cc engine and trim as per 848cc City (Chassis Number XL2S1O10 743114). Cost: £2,796.
October 1980: Mini 1000 Super discontinued and Mini 1000 HL launched with Clubman instruments, tinted glass, larger door bins and Metro four-spoke steering wheel (Chassis Number XL2S1N10 743004). Cost: £3,122. Mini Clubman Estate relaunched as Mini 1000 HL Estate (Chassis Number XL2W2010 751080). Cost: £3,761. All models now have Metro-type gear-lever knob and window handles, plus the Austin-Morris group badge on front grille. Saloons have new 'Mini' badge for bonnet.
February 1982: Last 1000 HL Estate bodyshell produced (final Chassis Number XL2W2010 V116099).
April 1982: Mini City redesignated Mini City E with higher final-drive ratio and high-compression head, and coachlines replaced with 'City' decals on doors and boot (Chassis Number XL2S1O10 V122249). 1000 HL saloon and estate given the same mechanical modifications and redesignated 1000 HLE. Cost: £2,999, £3,363 and £3,899 respectively. All models now with matt black bumpers.
September 1982: 1000 HLE redesignated

Mayfair, with Raschelle cloth trim, head restraints, cut-pile carpet and door casings, tinted glass and radio (Chassis Number XL2S1N10 V147144). Cost: £3,363. Estate withdrawn. City E given heated rear window, passenger sun visor, reversing lamps, black fuel filler cap.

October 1984: 12in wheels with low-profile tyres and front disc brakes, plus wheelarch spats standard for all models. Upholstery upgraded: City now with Sawtooth fabric and Mayfair with Chalkstripe velour.

September 1985: City E given colour-coded facia top roll, door handles, seat belts and instrument pack. Exterior trim (wheelarch extensions, grille and boot handle) now in grey instead of black.

November 1985: City E with twin adjustable

The Mini 1000 HL was launched in 1980 to replace the old 1000 Super. Externally, it had new badging and the plastic wheeltrims of the now defunct Clubman.

Inside the 1000 HL, the old centrally-mounted instrument binnacle gave way to the Clubman's two-dial pack mounted in front of the driver and there was a four-spoke steering wheel and padded dash top rail. Just visible are the new door bins and cloth check upholstery.

face-level air vents, twin instrument pack, four-spoke steering wheel, revised stalk control, vinyl-covered rear wheelarches, new wheeltrims, 'City' decals moved to rear quarter-panels. Mayfair given similar improvements except for a three-instrument nacelle including rev-counter, three-spoke colour-keyed soft-feel steering wheel, new gear knob, Needlefelt carpet inserts on facia and rear parcel shelf, revised trim for seats, door trims and rear-quarter casings, plus full-width wheeltrims with Austin Rover logo embossed. Both models gained extra indicators on front wings. Cost: £3,447 and £4,075 respectively.

October 1986: Rear-lap seat belts now standard.

June 1987: Austin badges deleted and replaced by new Mini badge on front grille.

August 1988: City E renamed City and now with different instrument graphics, front-seat head restraints and three-spoke steering wheel. Mayfair with stereo radio/cassette as standard and trim changes including new badging, new wheeltrims and Prism velour seat facings. Both models with driver's vanity mirror and rear seat belts as standard and engines with extra 1bhp (Chassis Number 396449).

October 1988: Brake servo now standard.

May 1989: John Cooper Performance Kit available as optional extra.

June 1989: Catalytic convertor available as optional extra (Chassis Number 426565).

November 1991: City gained full-width wheeltrims, chrome bumpers, Harlequin cloth

From April 1982, all Minis were treated to revised gearing and a high-compression cylinder head from the Metro HLE for improved fuel economy. All received an 'E' tag to denote the change. This is a Mini City E. Note the revised position of the grille badge and the replacement of the coachlines with a simple 'City' decal on the door.

Within months of the launch of the E-Type Mini, the HLE was renamed the Mayfair. Externally, it looked identical to the HLE except for its coachline, 'Mayfair' decals and extra door mirror.

The Mayfair, sold from 1982, was available with optional 10in alloy wheels, shown here. When these were specified, screw-on black plastic wheelarch extensions were necessary to cover the extra width.

0-60 IN ONE GALLON FLAT.

Specially adapted Metro HLE engines mean the new E-Type Minis get 60MPG and go 12,000 miles or one full year between services.

Test drive the new E-Type Minis. You won't believe how slow your money can go.

THE NEW E-TYPE MINIS.

AUSTIN

An advert for the economy Minis ("The New E-Type Minis") extolling their new-found 60mpg economy and extended service intervals.

trim. Mayfair given chrome-effect grille, body-coloured door mirrors and number-plate lamp, improved R652 stereo, new chrome 'Mayfair' bootlid badge. Both models with door pulls, window winders, steering wheel and column in black instead of grey (Chassis Number 034169).

May 1992: Production of City ceased, replaced by Mini Sprite. 998cc Mayfair replaced by 1.3-litre Mayfair. Final Chassis Number 049349.

Total production: 1,439,819 (excluding Mini 1000 HL Estate).

Inside the Mayfair, the trim was far more plush, with Raschelle cloth upholstery for the seats and doors and cut-pile carpets. With standard tinted glass, head restraints and radio, this was luxury on a grand scale by Mini standards.

In 1984, all Minis received front disc brakes and 12in wheels fitted with old 1275 GT-style trims. This is a facelifted 1985 Mini City E with yet another change of wheeltrims, extra side indicators, Nimbus grey exterior trim and 'City' decals moved to the rear wings. Note the reappearance of the Austin name on the grille.

In 1985, the famous single-dial instrument pod finally gave way to changing times in the City E. As part of a big interior spring-clean, it was replaced by the twin-dial square binnacle. Other changes visible in this picture included a four-spoke steering wheel, twin adjustable face vents and revised stalk control.

The Mayfair's interior from 1985 was much improved. The triple-instrument pack – first seen in the 1275 GT – included a rev-counter, there was a new three-spoke steering wheel and gear knob, plus new-style cloth for the seats.

In 1985, the Mayfair also received new wheeltrims, this time full-width with the Austin Rover logo embossed on them. It now had grey, not black, exterior trim and additional side flashers.

The optional alloy wheels available from 1984 – for the Mayfair only – were particularly smart and included a removable central panel embossed with the Austin Rover Group logo.

From 1988, the City E became just the City again and its graphics were revised accordingly.

The 1988 Mayfair also had a graphics overhaul, with a new 'Mayfair' logo. Also new were different full-width wheeltrims and velour upholstery for the seats.

With the Mini Clubman, a new upmarket Mini was created. The most striking difference was the nose: longer, squarer and uglier, it incorporated new lights, a new bumper, different bonnet and front wings and a new grille with a long vertical Mini badge.

The dashboard of the Clubman was very different from that of ordinary Minis. In particular, the instruments were now placed in an oblong box in front of the driver, offering readouts for speed, fuel level and water temperature. Face-level ventilation improved comfort and the three-spoke steering wheel was unique to the Clubman, as were the seats.

Mini Clubman and Mini Clubman Estate (1969–80)

Coinciding with the launch of the new MkIII Minis, and sharing their general improvements, BLMC launched the new Clubman and Clubman Estate in October 1969. The saloon slotted in as a more upmarket Mini, while the estate replaced the old Austin and Morris Mini estate cars.

Common to both new Clubmans was a completely revised nose. The front was extended and became squarer, a new chrome-trimmed grille with a different 'Mini' badge was fitted, the front bumper was unique to the model, the front lights were different and the bonnet and front wings

were redesigned to follow the revised contours. Other external identifying features were the six-spoked steel hubcaps – with optional bright wheeltrims – and boot-mounted Clubman badge.

In equipment, the Clubman was a parallel for the 1000 model (*ie* retaining the old Super De Luxe specification), but it had a new interior. There was a rectangular-shaped instrument binnacle sited ahead of the driver containing a speedometer on one side and a combined fuel gauge/water temperature gauge on the other. It also had face-level ventilation some seven years before the Mini 1000 and it boasted unique trim, special contoured seats and its own three-spoke steering wheel with a 'Clubman' badge in its centre.

The Estate also came with sliding rear windows as on the old Countryman/Traveller, but was never available with 'woody' rear bodywork. Instead, it came with vinyl-coated steel fake wood trims extending the length of the car (later replaced by contrasting coloured stripes). It also had driver's and passenger's side wing mirrors where the saloon had none until a single door mirror was standardized across the Mini range from 1973.

While the Estate continued with dry rubber-cone suspension, the Clubman saloon retained the Hydrolastic suspension abandoned by most other Minis. It finally gave way to dry rubber in 1971.

Automatic transmission was available on both versions, but when the 1,098cc engine was standardized on both models in 1975, an automatic Clubman could only be bought with a 998cc engine.

Apart from interior improvements and a minor

The early Clubman door trim was unique to the model. Like all Minis after 1969, it had winding windows and a lever-pull door release.

facelift in 1976, the Clubman had relatively few changes during its life. Post-1976 Clubmans could be easily identified by their new grille incorporating a cross pattern. The Clubman saloon disappeared in 1980 when the Mini Metro was introduced, but the estate car remained available in 998cc form only for a further two years, albeit rebadged as a Mini 1000 HL Estate (see above).

Specification

998cc

Engine	998cc 4-cyl OHV
Engine designation	99H
Bore/stroke	64.59 x 76.2mm
Compression ratio	8.3:1 (8.9:1 with automatic)
Power output	38bhp at 5,250rpm (41bhp at 4,850rpm)
Torque	52lb.ft at 2,700rpm (52lb.ft at 2,750rpm)
Transmission	Four-speed manual: Ratios: 4th 3.765, 3rd 5.317, 2nd 8.176, 1st 13.657 Four-speed automatic optional
Steering	Rack-and-pinion
Brakes	Drum/drum
Suspension	Saloon: Hydrolastic to 1971/rubber cones 1971–80 Estate: Rubber cones
Wheels	10 x 3.5in (12 x 4.5in Denovo optional from 1977 on saloon only)
Tyres	5.20 x 10in cross-ply; 145-10 radial-ply (from 1973)
Wheelbase	80.2in (2,036mm) Estate: 84.2in (2,139mm)
Length	124.6in (3,165mm) Estate: 133.9in (3,400mm)
Width	55.5in (1,410mm)
Height	53in (1,346mm)
Front track	48in (1,219mm)
Rear track	47.25in (1,200mm)
Weight	Saloon: 1,406lb (639kg) Estate: 1,514lb (687kg)

The Clubman front looked better balanced on the Estate car. The 'wood' trims down the sides of the car were in fact made of steel and covered with wood-effect vinyl. This made up for the fact that wooden battens for the rear half of the car were no longer available. Note the Clubman-only six-spoke hubcaps, supplemented here by optional wheeltrim embellishers.

The Estate's rear doors opened up usefully wide. This model is pictured in standard form, without the extra bright wheeltrims.

The rear doors of the Clubman Estate worked the same as the old Traveller/Countryman, but now had chrome-edged fake wood inserts. Note the new Clubman badging and the old-style rear lights, which carried on until the end of production.

Fuel tank	Saloon: 5.5gal (25l), 7.5gal (34l) from 1976
	Estate: 6.5gal (29.5l)
Luggage capacity	Saloon: 5.5cu ft (0.16cu m) – 4.1cu ft (0.116cu m) from 1976
	Estate: 18.5cu ft (0.52cu m) – seats raised; 35.3cu ft (1cu m) – seats folded

Specification 1,098cc

As Mini Clubman 998cc, except:

Engine	1,098cc four-cylinder OHV
Engine designation	10
Bore/stroke	64.59 x 83.73mm
Compression ratio	8.5:1
Power output	45bhp at 5,250rpm
Torque	56lb.ft at 2,700rpm
Transmission	Manual only
Suspension	Dry rubber cones
Weight	Saloon: 1,424lb (646kg)
	Estate: 1,458lb (661kg)
Fuel tank	Saloon: 7.5gal (34l)
Luggage capacity	Saloon: 4.1cu ft (0.116cu m)

Performance

	998cc	1,098cc
Maximum speed	75mph (121km/h)	82mph (132km/h)
0–50mph	14.1sec	12.4sec
0–60mph	21.0sec	17.9sec
30–50mph	12.0sec	11.8sec
40–60mph	25.8sec	14.0sec
50–70mph	29.2sec	21.1sec
Average fuel consumption	34mpg	37mpg
Government fuel test (Urban/56mph/75mph)	37.4/37.4/– (auto sal)	35.3/46.8/32.1 (sal)
	37.4/36.3/– (auto est)	34.8/45.4/33.7 (est)

Space in the back of the Estate was as generous as ever and the layout was essentially unchanged. The materials used to trim the interior were the only difference from the early Mini estates.

Optional extras

Automatic transmission (998cc engine only)
Rake-adjustable front seats (until 1975)
Heated rear window (saloon only – until 1974)
Wheeltrims (until 1976)
Rear bumper overriders (saloon only – until 1971)
Radial tyres (until 1973)
Steering column lock
Metallic paint (saloon only – from 1977)
Denovo wheel and tyres (saloon only – from 1977)

Range

Mini Clubman (998cc) (1969–80)
Mini Clubman Estate (998cc) (1969–80)
Mini Clubman (1,098cc) (1975–80)
Mini Clubman Estate (1,098cc) (1975–80)

Production history

May 1969: Mini Clubman saloon production began (Chassis Number X/A2S2 101).
September 1969: Mini Clubman Estate

MOC 211R

All Clubmans were given a minor facelift in 1976. The front grille was new, with a cross pattern containing a Leyland Cars logo and 'Mini' script. The special hubcaps were ditched, although the bright wheel embellishers remained available – for one year, until new plastic wheeltrims were substituted.

production began (Chassis Number X/A2W2 576).

October 1969: Mini Clubman saloon and Estate announced. Cost: £720 and £763 respectively.

October 1970: Steering lock introduced.

June 1971: Suspension on saloon changed from Hydrolastic to rubber cones (from Commission Number S20S-48645A). Improved CV driveshaft boot.

February 1972: Improved synchromesh from engine 99H 353EH 275337.

April 1972: Split-type needle-roller bearings on idler gears.

December 1972: Alternator standard.

February 1973: Radial-ply tyres standard.

April 1973: Rod-shift gearchange introduced.

June 1973: Plunging CV joints on inboard ends of new driveshafts and improved door check bracket fitted.

August 1973: Single door mirror replaced wing mirrors on Estate.

February 1974: Inertia-reel seat belts standard.

June 1974: Heated rear window standard on saloon, twin-silencer exhaust fitted on both models. (New chassis numbering system: Chassis Number XL2S2 and XL2W2 101).

October 1975: Cloth seat trim and reclining front seats standard. Seat belt anchorages relocated to rear side bins (Chassis Number XL2S2 255178 – saloon, and XL2W2 255208 – Estate). 88°

thermostat standard. Manual versions of 998cc-engined cars discontinued (final Chassis Numbers: XL2S2 258876 – saloon, and XL2W2 259638 – Estate). 998cc-engined versions continued with automatic transmission only, and standard manual-gearbox engine became 1,098cc.

May 1976: New black grille with two horizontal bars and cross-shaped motif with new Mini badge in centre. Twin column-mounted control stalks fitted, new rocker-switch type panel incorporating hazard lights standard, larger pedals from Allegro, moulded carpets and ignition/steering lock from BL Princess fitted. Suspension modified with softer rear springs and damper settings (saloon only), plus new subframe mounts (Chassis Number XL2S2 341660 – saloon, and XL2W2 330503 – Estate).

July 1977: New wheeltrims, leather-bound steering wheel, lockable fuel cap, reversing lights and tinted glass standard (Chassis Number XC2S2 454689 – saloon, and XC2W2 455434 – Estate). Estate with painted stripes down flanks instead of mock wood.

August 1980: Mini Clubman models discontinued (final Chassis Numbers XC2S200 741783 – saloon, and XC2W200 751088 – Estate).

Total production: Saloon, approx 275,583; Estate (incl 1000 HL Estate), approx 197,606. Total: approx 473,189.

After 1977, the Clubman Estate traded in its mock wood trim for painted stripes. From the same time, Clubmans became available with Denovo wheels and run-flat tyres as an optional extra (pictured here). They enabled you to continue gently to your destination, but had an adverse effect on handling.

The Mini 1275 GT at launch in October 1969. It shared the Clubman nose, and a number of features made it the most sporty-looking Mini to date: Rostyle 4.5in steel wheels, special grille, bold contrasting coloured stripes with 'Mini 1275 GT' decals and a choice of body colours unique to the GT.

The grille of the 1275 GT was basically the same as on the Clubman, but only the top and bottom bars were chromed, the rest remaining black. A special red 'GT' badge appeared on the nearside.

Mini 1275 GT (1969–80)

As the Mini-Cooper MkII was taken out of production, a replacement was found in the 1275 GT, launched alongside the Mini Clubman and Mini MkIII models in October 1969.

Based on the Mini Clubman bodyshell, it shared all of the Clubman's major facelift details. Its distinguishing external features were a blacked-out front grille containing a red GT badge, wide Rostyle steel wheels from the MG Midget – with standard radial-ply tyres – and prominent contrasting-colour stripes above the sill line with 'Mini 1275 GT' decals and identifying rear badgework.

Inside, the 1275 GT differed from the Clubman in having new-style seat coverings, a three-instrument binnacle – the extra dial being a rev-counter – and a leather-bound steering wheel with a '1275 GT' logo in the boss.

The 1275 GT used the single-carburettor 1,275cc A-series engine with a close-ratio four-speed gearbox. Front disc brakes from the Mini-Cooper 'S' were fitted as standard. Like the Clubman saloon, the 1275 GT used Hydrolastic suspension at first, before reverting to the dry rubber type in 1971.

The 1275 GT became the first production Mini to be fitted with wheels larger than the 10in variety in 1974 with 12in wheels and larger brake discs. Denovo wheels and run-flat tyres were offered as an option from this time, then made standard in 1977.

Along with the Clubman saloon, the 1275 GT was phased out on the introduction of the Mini Metro in 1980.

Specification

As Mini Clubman, except:

Engine	1,275cc four-cylinder OHV
Engine designation	12H
Bore/stroke	70.64 x 81.33mm
Compression ratio	8.3:1 (low compression)
	8.8:1 (high compression)
Power output	59bhp at 5,300rpm (54bhp from 1974)
Torque	65lb.ft at 2,550rpm
Transmission	Four-speed manual only: Ratios: 4th 3.65, 3rd 5.22, 2nd 8.10, 1st 12.87 From 1970: Ratios: 4th 3.44, 3rd 4.92, 2nd 7.63, 1st 12.13
Brakes	Disc/drum
Wheels	10 x 4.5in alloy 12 x 4.5in (from 1974) 310mm Dunlop Denovo (from 1977)

Fitting in with its racy image, the 1275 GT was the first Mini to get a rev-counter, installed in an extended three-dial version of the Clubman nacelle. The steering wheel was leather-bound and had a '1275 GT' boss, while there was fitted carpeting and special 'competition class' seating.

The 1275 GT was the first Mini to be fitted with 12in wheels, a change which occurred in 1974. At the same time, larger, non-servo front discs were fitted.

Tyres	Dunlop 145-10in	Rear track	47.25in (1,200mm)
	Dunlop SP 145/70-12in (from 1974)	Weight	1,476lb (670kg)
		Fuel tank	5.5gal (25l) – 7.5gal (34l) from 1974
	Dunlop Denovo 155/65SR-310 run-flat (from 1977)	Luggage capacity	5.5cu ft (0.16cu m) – 4.1cu ft
Front track	48in (1,219mm)		(0.116cu m) from 1974

Performance

	(1969)	(1971)	(1974)
Maximum speed	86mph (138km/h)	90mph (145km/h)	86mph (138km/h)
0–50mph	10.2sec	9.3sec	10.0sec
0–60mph	14.7sec	13.3sec	14.6sec
30–50mph	9.1sec	8.5sec	10.2sec
40–60mph	10.5sec	9.8sec	11.5sec
50–70mph	–	12.2sec	14.9sec
Average fuel consumption	30mpg	35mpg	35mpg
Government fuel test (Urban/56mph/75mph)	–	–	34.7/46.0/33.3

81

Optional extras

As Clubman, except:
Laminated windscreen
Denovo wheels and tyres (from 1974 – standard
   from 1977)

Note: Automatic transmission, radial tyres and
   wheeltrims not available as options.

Range

Mini 1275 GT (1969–80)

Production history

As Mini Clubman, except:
October 1969: Mini 1275 GT introduced (Chassis
Number X/AD2 107). Cost: £834.

Coinciding with the Clubman's facelift in 1976, the 1275 GT was given the same new grille as the Clubman, and a 'GT' badge was no longer fitted. This is a 1977 Leyland publicity shot showing a new front spoiler suitable for the Clubman and 1275 GT.

Improvements to the 1275 GT interior in 1976 included new striped seats, dipping rear-view mirror, a vanity mirror in the passenger's and a ticket pocket in the driver's sun visor, door pockets, handbrake grip, new steering wheel, new rocker switch panel and an additional mirror on the passenger's door.

December 1970: Final-drive ratio changed from
3.65:1 to 3.44:1 (Engine Number 12H 389 SH
6901).
December 1971: Improved driveshaft CV boot.
February 1972: Improved synchromesh from
Engine Number 12H 353 EH 22958.
May 1974: Temperature-controlled air intake
system now fitted (power output now 54bhp).
June 1974: Larger non-servo front disc brakes
fitted with larger 12in wheels, plus new 7.5gal fuel
tank (new numbering system: Chassis Number
XE2D2 101).

May 1976: Changes as Clubman, plus old GT
badge deleted from grille, new striped seats,
passenger's vanity mirror, door pockets,
passenger's door mirror and handbrake grip
(Chassis Number XE2D2 342896).
August 1977: Denovo wheels and tyres standard
(Chassis Number XE2D2 455914).
October 1979: Black door mirrors and rain gutter
standard.
August 1980: Mini 1275 GT discontinued (final
Chassis Number XE2D200 744571).
Total production: 110,673.

The final major change for the 1275 GT was the standard-ization of Denovo wheels and tyres in 1977 – they had already been optional for three years. The wisdom of fitting run-flat tyres – which gave poorer roadholding – to the performance version of the Mini was questioned by many and most GTs were converted back to standard tyres by disapproving owners.

Mini Sprite and Mini Mayfair [1,275cc] (1992 to date)

After a production run of over 30 years, the 998cc-engined Minis were finally replaced in 1992 with models driven by a less powerful version of the catalyzed 1,275cc carburettor A-series unit used in the Rover Metro.

The old City was replaced by a new entry-level model, the Sprite, a name first used on a Mini special edition of 1983. This shared almost all of the equipment of the old City, but now had full-width steel wheeltrims, black wheelarch extensions, chrome bumpers and a chrome Mini badge on the bootlid. A 'Sprite' logo was placed on the rear body flanks.

The 1992 Mini Mayfair now had a chrome-effect grille, a contrasting-coloured coachline (without a 'Mayfair' logo), revised chromed badging and body-colour door mirrors. The same wheeltrims as the Sprite were standard, with Cooper-style Minilite-type alloys available as an option. The interior was in Chevron velour, whereas the Sprite made do with Harlequin cloth, and the old distinction of a two-instrument pack for the Mayfair was preserved.

From 1993, the Mayfair's interior was thor-oughly spruced-up with a full-width burr-walnut dashboard with three dials set in a slightly raised plinth, a radio/cassette player in the centre of the dash – rather than above the passenger's knees, as before – and a clock above that.

At the same time, both models received bigger front seats from the Metro, new badges, VIN chassis code-etched glass and, for the first time since 1959, an internal bonnet release, all in the interest of added security. To underline the point, the Mayfair gained a standard alarm/engine immobilizer.

Specification

Engine	1,275cc four-cylinder OHV
Engine designation	12
Bore/stroke	70.64 x 81.33mm
Compression ratio	10.5:1
Power output	50bhp at 5,000rpm
Torque	66lb.ft at 2,600rpm
Transmission	Four-speed manual: Ratios: 4th 3.11, 3rd 4.43, 2nd 6.795, 1st 11.34, Rev 11.40 Optional four-speed automatic: Ratios: 4th 3.76, 3rd 5.49, 2nd 6.94, 1st 10.11, Rev 10.11
Steering	Rack-and-pinion
Brakes	Disc/drum
Suspension	Independent front/rear with rubber cones
Wheels	12 x 4.5in steel
Tyres	145/70 SR-12 low-profile radial-ply
Wheelbase	80.1in (2,035mm)
Length	120.25in (3,054mm)
Width	55.5in (1,410mm)
Height	53.25in (1,353mm)
Front track	48.8in (1,240mm)
Rear track	47.6in (1,210mm)
Weight	1,375lb (625kg)
Fuel tank	7.5gal (34l)
Luggage capacity	4.1cu ft (0.116cu m)

The old Austin Sprite name was revived for the new 1,275cc base model from 1992. Apart from its engine, the Sprite's specification basically continued that of the old City. The new model, though, received Mayfair-style wheeltrims, chrome bumpers, black wheelarch spats, a new chrome Mini badge on the boot and new 'Sprite' graphics treatment.

Performance

	Manual	Automatic
Maximum speed	87mph (140km/h)	82mph (132km/h)
0–50mph	–	
0–60mph	13.4sec	16.5sec
30–50mph	10.9sec	–
40–60mph	–	–
50–70mph	14.9sec	–
Average fuel consumption	36mpg	33mpg
Government fuel test (Urban/56mph/75mph)	37.3/54.2/33.8	35.5/46.8/30.7

The 1992 Mayfair was even more similar to the outgoing model than the Sprite. New features to move it more upmarket included the neat Cooper chrome-effect grille and body-coloured door mirrors. In place of the standard wheeltrims (the same as the Sprite's), the optional smart spoked alloy wheels *a la* Mini-Cooper could be ordered, as pictured here.

From 1993, the Mayfair received a significant interior refit. Gone was the old separate instrument binnacle, to be replaced by a smart Cabriolet-style burr-walnut dashboard with glovebox, hi-fi and analogue clock installed. Also new were cloth front seats from the Metro.

Optional extras
Automatic transmission
Alarm and engine immobilizer (Sprite only)
Leather upholstery
Alloy wheels (Mayfair only)
Metallic, pearlescent or black paintwork
Rubber mats
Fabric mats
Load liner
Sunroof
Handbrake grip
Door bins
Sump guard
Rear mudflaps

Passenger's door mirror (Sprite only)
Driving lamps
Locking wheelnuts
Locking petrol cap
Wheeltrims
Bonnet stripes
Chrome rocker cover/studs
Radio (Sprite only)
Superior radio/cassette systems

Range
Mini Sprite (1992 to date)
Mini Mayfair (1992 to date)

Production history

May 1992: New Mini Sprite launched to replace City, with 1.3-litre carburettor engine, also shared by new Mayfair, which received chrome-effect grille and new chrome badges (Chassis Number 049349).

May 1993: Both models now with new Metro-type front seats, internal bonnet release and VIN chassis code-etched front and rear screens. Sprite given passenger door mirror, front door bins, boot mat and new trim. Mayfair also given alarm, full-width walnut facia and locking wheelnuts.

Total production: (to end of April 1994): 35,423.

Mini-Cooper (1990 to date)

The first official Rover involvement with a Nineties' Mini-Cooper was the availability of the John Cooper Performance Conversion Kit for the Mini in Rover dealerships from May 1989. This was based on the standard 998cc engine and consisted of twin SU carburettors, a Janspeed cylinder head, bigger inlet valves, 9.75:1 compression ratio, hardened valve inserts, twin-box exhaust and 3.1:1 final drive. Power output was 64bhp and the conversion cost £995 plus tax and fitting charges.

However, the official new Rover Mini-Cooper was launched in July 1990. This was based on the specification of the luxury Mini Thirty special edition, but employed the 1,275cc catalyst-equipped A-series engine lately used in the MG Metro. Developing 61bhp, it was the quickest Mini made since the original Mini-Cooper 'S' left production in 1971.

In its first limited edition of 1,650 cars, the Mini-Cooper came with a pair of white bonnet stripes plus a 'John Cooper' signature. Body colours were green, red or black with, of course, a white roof. Sparked alloy wheels were standard, as were a glass sunroof, auxiliary driving lamps, door mirrors, a chrome grille, winged Cooper bonnet badge and chrome bumpers. Inside there was black leather trim and a red steering wheel.

As launched in production form, the Mini-Cooper resembled the commemorative special edition closely, but was sold without spotlamps, bonnet stripes or sunroof to keep costs down. The wing mirrors now matched the roof colour. The interior was also more sombre, with cloth trim and black carpets and steering wheel.

From 1991, Rover marketed a John Cooper-developed performance tuning kit to turn the Cooper into an 'S'.

The sigil for the tuned Cooper 'S' package.

The Mini-Cooper became a regular production model from September 1990, minus the white bonnet stripes, sunroof, signatures and spotlamps and with cloth trim, black carpet (the special edition had red) and black steering wheel. Thus it was a little cheaper to buy (although you could still opt for the driving lamps, sunroof and bonnet stripes – with or without the Cooper signature – as extras). The door mirrors now matched the roof colour and the standard stereo was mounted in front of the passenger.

John Cooper developed a Rover-approved conversion kit to make a Mini-Cooper 'S', available from March 1991. This had an air cooler and an engine developing 78bhp, while the handling package added low-profile tyres and adjustable shock absorbers.

To comply with emissions laws, the Mini-Cooper was treated to a three-way-controlled catalyst-

Only a year into the reborn Cooper's production life, its carburettor engine was swapped for a fuel-injected unit. Coinciding with this change, the Cooper's specification moved up closer to the original edition's: standard spotlamps, bonnet stripes, red carpets and leather seat trim. A chrome '1.3i' badge on the bootlid further distinguished the revised car.

equipped single-point fuel-injected 1,275cc Metro engine in 1991. The Cooper 1.3i was easily distinguished by its reversion to white bonnet stripes and had improved interior trim with 'Lightning' seat facings incorporating leather trim, red piping in the seats and doors, red-stitched steering wheel and red carpets. It gained an R652 hi-fi system and a '1.3i' badge on the boot. Again there was a factory-warranted John Cooper Performance Conversion, revised to suit the fuel-injected engine. This became known as the Mini-Cooper Si. As the Cooper matured, it could be bought in colours other than green, red or black. White Diamond, Storm Grey and Quicksilver also became available, in which case the roof was painted black, not white.

Specification

As Mini Sprite/Mayfair, except:

	Mini-Cooper Carb	Mini-Cooper S Carb
Compression ratio	10.5:1	10.25:1
Power output	61bhp at 5,550rpm	78bhp at 6,000rpm
Torque	61lb.ft at 3,000rpm	78lb.ft at 3,250rpm
Transmission	Four-speed manual only: Ratios: As Mini Sprite	4th 3.44, 3rd 4.93, 2nd 7.63, 1st 12.13
Brakes	Disc/drum	Disc/drum
Wheels	12 x 4.5in	12 x 4.5in
Tyres	Dunlop SP Sport 165/60 R12	
Front track	49.2in (1,250mm)	49.2in (1,250mm)
Rear track	47.4in (1,205mm)	47.4in (1,205mm)
Weight	1,530lb (695kg)	1,556lb (706kg)

Performance

Maximum speed	87mph (139km/h)	97mph (156km/h)
0–50mph	8.5sec	7.6sec
0–60mph	12.2sec	11.0sec
30–50mph	–	9.6sec
40–60mph	–	10.1sec
50–70mph	16.9sec	12.7sec
Average fuel consumption	33mpg	27mpg
Government fuel test (Urban/56mph/75mph)	37.4/49.4/38.8	–

Specification

As Mini-Cooper Carb, except:

	Mini-Cooper 1.3i	Mini-Cooper Si
Engine	Fuel-injection	Fuel-injection
Compression ratio	10.0:1	10.5:1
Power output	63bhp at 5,700rpm	77bhp at 5,800rpm
Torque	70lb.ft at 3,900rpm	80lb.ft at 3,000rpm
Wheels	12 x 4.5in	12 x 4.5in
Tyres	Pirelli 145/70 R12	Dunlop SP Sport 165/60 R12

Performance

Maximum speed	92mph (148km/h)	100mph (161km/h)
0–60mph	11.5sec	10.0sec
30–50mph	9.8sec	–
50–70mph	12.4sec	11.0sec
Average fuel consumption	32mpg	27mpg
Government fuel test (Urban/56mph/75mph)	36.6/48.9/33.6	–

Inside the Mini-Cooper 1.3i, luxury met sporting appeal. The seats were trimmed in Lightning material with leather sides, there was red piping in the seats and a red Mylar strip for the doors and rear-quarter casings, red-stitched leather steering wheel, red carpet, red needles for the instruments and sophisticated hi-fi equipment.

Optional extras

Spotlights (1990–91)
Sunroof
Sump guard
Bonnet stripes (1990–91)
John Cooper Performance Conversion Kit
Rear mudflaps with Cooper logo
Tyre valve caps with Cooper logo
Metallic paint
Wood-rim steering wheel
Burr walnut full-width facia
Fabric mats with Cooper logo
Superior stereo system
'Italian Job' pack (twin spotlamps, bonnet stripes, moulded boot liner – from 1991)
'RAC Rally' pack (as 'Italian Job' pack, plus tinted glass, sunroof and mudflaps – from 1991)
'Monte Carlo' pack (as 'RAC Rally' pack, plus sump guard, locking wheelnuts and fire extinguisher – from 1991)
Monte Carlo anniversary kit (extra auxiliary lamps, white racing patches, 'Monte Carlo Rally' decals, coachline – from 1994)

Range

Mini-Cooper (1990–91)
Mini-Cooper 1.3i (1991 to date)

Production history

May 1989: John Cooper Garages offered Rover-approved Mini-Cooper performance conversion kit for 998cc Mini in UK.

July 1990: Mini-Cooper limited edition launched by Rover with 1,275cc catalyzed engine, white bonnet stripes with 'John Cooper' signature and luxury trim (Chassis Number 100001). Cost: £6,995.

September 1990: Mini-Cooper launched as official Rover production model, with more basic trim and no bonnet stripes (Chassis Number XNCADH 100098). Cost: £6,595.

March 1991: Performance kit for Mini-Cooper launched to create new Mini-Cooper 'S'. Cost: £1,751. Handling pack also available for an extra £671.

October 1991: Mini-Cooper 1.3i replaced carburettor model with fuel-injected three-way-catalyzed engine, spotlamps and superior trim (Chassis Number XNCADH 031550). Cost: £7,845.

March 1992: 'Si' John Cooper Performance Kit available from John Cooper Garages.

March 1993: Now with VIN code etched onto front and rear screens, standard passenger door mirror, internal bonnet release, new front seats, door bins and boot mat. Alarm/engine immobilizer fitted.

January 1994: Monte Carlo dress-up kit offered as an option.

Total production: Mini-Cooper (commemorative model): 1,650; Mini-Cooper (carburettor model): 19,899; Mini-Cooper 1.3i: 21,034 (to end of April 1994).

Mini Cabriolet (1993 to date)

Like the Mini-Cooper, the Cabriolet began life as a limited edition. In June 1991, Rover approved a conversion effected by a German Rover dealer called LAMM Autohaus. This was based on the Mini-Cooper, but had Mini Mayfair trim, a wood dash and a full body styling kit. Only 75 right-hand-drive examples were made available to British customers through Rover dealers in 1991, and they quickly sold out.

The production Rover Mini Cabriolet made its debut at the October 1992 Birmingham International Motor Show. Unlike the limited-edition model, this version was developed jointly by Rover Special Products and Karmann of Germany to a very different design and was built entirely at Longbridge.

The roof was chopped off and substantial reinforcement added to the bodyshell. The manually-operated colour-coded hood was a simple one-piece mechanism with twin catches and a plastic rear window. When folded, it stacked up behind the rear seats and a cover – normally stored in the boot – would then protect it. The rear quarter-windows described an arc to withdraw completely into the body.

The Cabriolet was mechanically almost identical to the Cooper 1.3i, but added such items as five-spoke Revolution alloy wheels with a 'Mini' logo in their centre – plus lockable wheelnuts –

The production Mini Cabriolet was the most lavish Mini yet seen: a full bodykit, Revolution five-spoke alloy wheels and plenty of chrome. The hood folded back to form a high back behind the rear seats and the specially-designed rear quarter-windows could be wound down out of sight.

Easily the most luxurious Mini yet offered, the Cabriolet boasted an interior with burr-walnut full-width dash, door inserts and pulls and gear knob, tinted windows, leather steering wheel, steel sill covering with 'Cabriolet' script, clock, rev-counter, stereo, cut-pile carpet and special rake-adjustable sports seats with Chevron facings and head restraints.

and a full colour-coded bodykit, including a deep front bumper/spoiler, faired-in wheelarches, side skirts and a matching rear bumper. The door handles, number-plate lamp cover and boot handle were chromed and chrome spotlamps were fitted as standard.

Two colours were available: Caribbean Blue with a grey hood or Nightfire Red with a red hood. There were special identifying Cabriolet badges.

Inside the Cabriolet was a paragon of luxury: the dashboard was entirely covered in burr-walnut with three inset instruments and a clock, plus wooden door cappings, gear-lever knob and door pulls. There was a leather steering wheel, standard analogue clock, cut-pile carpeting, colour-keyed seat belts and chrome kick-plates. Strangely, the specially-designed front seats were non-tilting and they were covered with new Chevron trim. Standard security equipment included a full volumetric and perimetric alarm system, coded stereo, locking fuel cap and VIN-etched glass.

Specification
As Mini-Cooper 1.3i, except:

Wheels	12 x 5B Revolution cast alloys
Tyres	165/60 R12 low-profile
Length	121.65in (3,090mm)
Width	62.2in (1,580mm)
Height	53.7in (1,364mm)
Front track	51.6in (1,310mm)
Rear track	49in (1,245mm)
Weight	1,650lb (750kg)

Performance

Maximum speed	92mph (148km/h)	
0–50mph	–	
0–60mph	12.3sec	
30–50mph	10.5sec	
40–60mph	–	
50–70mph	13.3sec	
Average fuel consumption	32mpg	
Government fuel test (Urban/56mph/75mph)	36.5/50.2/34.3mpg	

Optional extras
As Mini Sprite/Mayfair, except:
Power-operated hood
NB. Rubber mats not available

Range
Mini Cabriolet (1993 to date)

Production history
June 1991: Mini Cabriolet announced as a Rover-approved limited-edition built by LAMM Autohaus, with Mayfair-style seats and trim, Mini-Cooper mechanicals, body styling kit (Chassis Number XNWBMH 024857). Cost: £12,250.
October 1992: Production version of Rover Mini Cabriolet given public debut.
July 1993: Cabriolet available to public with fuel-injected Mini-Cooper engine, superior interior fittings and driving lamps (Chassis Number XNWBMH 061481). Cost: £11,995.
Total production: Mini Cabriolet (LAMM): 75; Mini Cabriolet (Rover): 414 (to end of April 1994).

SECTION FIVE

Mini Special Editions

Inside the 1976 "limited edition striped seat Mini 1000", as the Leyland press release described it. The then reigning Miss Great Britain, Sue Cuff, tries out the model's MGB-style orange-striped brushed nylon seating.

What a strange phenomenon is the 'special edition' or 'limited edition': a spruced-up version of a production model, given a suitably exotic or characterful name and produced in a 'strictly limited' batch. Everyone is now all-too familiar with them.

BMC was probably responsible for launching the first ever special edition car with the Morris Minor 1,000,000. It was followed by many other manufacturers, notably Volkswagen, in the Seventies, but the real heyday of the limited edition was not until the spoilt-for-choice Eighties.

The idea of tailored, limited-production Minis had already been tried out in Europe with several varieties of Mini Special. The first British Mini special edition came as early as 1976. This initial foray into a potentially very lucrative arena was something of an out-of-time anomaly. The 1100S of 1979 and Sprite of 1983 would show the way far more clearly, as Minis led a veritable special edition boom in the Eighties.

Few other cars can have come in as many limited-production guises as the Mini. The galaxy of fashionable and suggestive names is bewildering: Ritz, Piccadilly, Sprite, Advantage, Neon, Designer, Racing, Tahiti, Sky, Check Mate and on and on…

This begs the question: Why? It is all down to marketing, of course. Limited Edition models have a high profile, inspire consumer imagination and pamper the buyer with a feast of little 'extras' for a 'bargain' price. Typically, this would consist of a paint job with appropriate graphics, a jazzier type of cloth for the interior and a couple of extra items of equipment, all packaged under an exotic name.

Alec Issigonis' regard for marketing men was about the same as that for bureaucrats and his disapproval of such glitz and frippery was very tangible, although in his retirement he never made an official comment about what Austin Rover was doing to his beloved Mini.

To many other eyes, the idea of dressing up Minis was anathema. Rowan Atkinson wrote in *Car* magazine in 1991 that special edition Minis were "merely applications of make-up to what was perceived as a tired old face, when in fact the Mini has elegant, classical features that are ruined by crude face paint. Mini Cock-Ups, the lot of them".

Yet they were certainly successful: up to a third of annual Mini sales during the late Eighties was taken up by special edition Minis. Typically, the buyers were women aged between 20 and 35. The fact that Minis became truly fashionable once more during the Eighties is probably greatly due to the success of the various special editions.

Another point worth making in their favour is that special editions were often the prototypes for changes which eventually made their way into regular production. For example, the Sprite had a triple-instrument binnacle before the Mayfair, and the first Mini to be fitted with 12in wheels and disc front brakes was the Mini 25; the Mini-Cooper and Cabriolet were launched as special editions before entering regular production.

From the start, each special edition always sold out. The first true Mini special edition, the 1100S, even had to have its intended production

The first 'real' Mini special edition was the 1100 Special. This was based on the Belgian-built regular production Mini 1100 Special with its 1,098cc engine and 'Special' badging, but the limited edition was built at Longbridge – the only 1.1-litre Mini with a standard bodyshell ever constructed in Britain. This is the Silver version with its black vinyl roof...

run doubled to cope with demand. Such was their popularity, abroad as well as in Britain, that Rover was soon releasing one new edition per year – sometimes more. In its bumper years, the 30th anniversary of 1989 and the following year, no less than 10 different names were launched for the Mini.

Two bizarre limited editions – just one car of each! – were made by Rover in 1993 to donate to the *Comic Relief* TV charity. One was a *Mr Bean* Mini, a replica of the green Mini seen in the TV series of the same name, and the other was the *Tomato* Mini, designed along the 'splatt' theme of that year's programme.

Quite apart from the special editions sold on the British market, there were several unique foreign-market-only editions, as described in *SECTION NINE: International Minis.*

Although the production runs of limited editions are easing, there is no end in sight. The arrival of a new special edition is now at least a twice-yearly event. Each one is eagerly snapped up by a public with an insatiable thirst for the marketing men's designs on their pay-packet. Despite the disapproval voiced in many quarters, they will undoubtedly become 'collectable' in Mini circles in years to come.

...and this is the Rose metallic version with its tan vinyl roof. Standard exterior features of the 1100 Special included graduated body stripes, wide alloy wheels, wheelarch extensions, small Mini garland motifs on the front wings, extra side indicators, Clubman bumpers, twin door mirrors, tinted glass and special badging.

Mini Limited Edition 1000 (1976)

The first attempt at a British-market special edition Mini was the Limited Edition 1000, introduced in January 1976. Judged by the extravagances of future special editions, this was a remarkably tame one.

It was externally distinguishable by its green-and-white paintwork with a gold coachline and chrome door mirrors. Inside, there was MGB-style orange striped brushed nylon trim, which sounds like the most dreadful colour clash. There were also special carpets, face-level ventilation and reclining seats, none of which yet featured on the 1000 model. The cost was £1,406, and 3,000 were made.

Mini 1100 Special (1979)

The first true special edition Mini celebrated 20 years of Mini production. The 1100 Special (or just 1100S) was an upmarket limited-production edition based on the standard 1000 bodyshell, but fitted with the 45bhp 1,098cc engine from the Clubman – the only 1.1-litre standard-bodyshell Mini ever made or sold in Britain.

Launched in August 1979, it looked far from being a standard Mini, with a choice of Silver or Rose metallic paintwork, shaded body stripes,

wide 5 x 10in alloy wheels with fatter Dunlop SP Sport 165/70 tyres, matt black wheelarch spats and wipers, extra indicators on the front wings, deeper Clubman-type bumpers, twin door mirrors, tinted glass, locking filler cap and a vinyl roof (in black with Silver paintwork, or light tan with Rose). To top it all, there were little 'Special' badges on the bootlid and in the front grille, as imported from Belgium.

Inside, the model received a sports steering wheel and the triple-instrument facia and centre console of the 1275 GT, which contained a standard radio, clock, lighter and oddments tray, plus an extra underslung tray on the passenger's side. The seats were upholstered in tartan check with colour co-ordinated cut-pile carpeting.

With the bigger engine, performance was superior to the standard Mini 1000 of the day: a top speed of 84mph and a 0–60mph time of 16.6sec were possible.

At a price of £3,300, a limited run of 2,500 cars was envisaged, but the popularity of the model soon persuaded BL to extend that to 5,000; the final production tally in fact reached 5,100.

Mini Sprite (1983)

The Mini Sprite was an important official special edition – released after a long gap in October 1983 – in anticipation of the 25th anniversary of the Mini. Its name revived the old Austin-Healey name last used in 1971. As there was already

The interior of the 1100 Special borrowed from the 1275 GT, including its triple instrument pack. There was a unique steering wheel with a Mini garland in the boss, a centre console incorporating a radio, clock and cigar lighter, plus an extra oddments tray above the passenger's feet. The tartan check seats were unique to the 1100S.

The 1983 Mini Sprite was essentially a dolled-up Mini City, pitched in price just below the more upmarket Mayfair. Some features, like the alloy wheels, twin door mirrors and triple instrument pack, were carried over from the 1979 special edition, but the 'Sprite' graphics were new.

a luxury Mini in the standard line-up (the Mayfair), the policy with the Sprite was to create a model pitched between the basic City and the Mayfair. Hence the Sprite was basically a spruced-up City.

It came in either Cinnabar Red or Primula Yellow and was immediately identifiable by its black side stripes incorporating a 'Sprite' logo on the rear flanks. It had twin door mirrors and wide

alloy wheels shod with 165/70 tyres, plus wheel spats.

Inside, there was a Mayfair facia with top roll and side vents, a three-instrument pack – before it became standard on the Mayfair – black PVC head restraints, grey herringbone-pattern seat facings, black vinyl trim and a four-spoke steering wheel. The cost was £3,334 and the total production run was 2,500 examples.

Mini 25 (1984)

Then the Mini limited editions came thick and fast. The 25th birthday of the Mini was a good excuse to launch a Silver Jubilee anniversary model, the Mini 25, in July 1984. It was based on the Mayfair and was the most luxuriously appointed Mini yet made.

The 25th anniversary Mini was, of course, painted silver and had a grey-and-red coachline with identifying 'Mini 25' decals on the rear flanks, boot and the centres of the wheels. The

For the Mini's 25th anniversary, Austin Rover created a true luxury Mini. The silver-painted '25' was most notable, perhaps, for its pioneering use of 1275 GT-style 12in wheels and front disc brakes. There were '25' logos in the wheel centres, body sides and bootlid.

A triple instrument binnacle, leather-bound steering wheel and standard stereo radio/cassette graced the opulent interior of the '25'. Just visible are the neat zippered pockets in front of each seat. The grey velvet upholstery for the seats, doors and rear-quarter casings was matched by grey-and-red carpets.

wheels were historic in a way: they were special 12in items fitted with disc brakes, and were seen on the Mini 25 several months in advance of their universal fitment to all Minis. The wheelarch spats, bumpers, door handles, grille and twin mirrors were all colour-coded in Nimbus grey.

Inside, the '25' had a leather-bound three-spoke steering wheel, grey-and-red carpets, Flint velvet trim with red piping for the seats, head restraints and rear quarter and door casings, with 'Mini 25' motifs on both front seat squabs. Ahead of each front seat cushion there were zip pockets. The luxury extended to cut-pile carpets, carpeted kick

strips, leather-bound red-stitched steering wheel – with a '25' motif in its boss – and red seat belts. There was a triple-instrument pack, including a rev-counter, and a standard stereo radio/cassette with twin rear speakers. Additional equipment included tinted glass, twin door mirrors and reversing and rear foglights.

The '25' cost £3,865 and was released in a limited edition of 5,000, of which 1,500 were exported. Despite the sizeable production run, Austin Rover reported that demand considerably exceeded supply. In France, the edition was known as the Mini 25 Anniversary.

The Mini Ritz of 1985 was a lightly dressed-up City with metallic silver paint and red striping and decals. Standard equipment included smart alloy wheels, colour-coded grey exterior trim and a fair bit of chroming.

The seats of the Ritz were perhaps its best feature: lusciously trimmed in contrasting red, blue and grey velvet, with standard headrests and 'Ritz' logos. Many of the interior parts were colour-keyed in a matching shade of blue.

Mini Ritz (1985)

By now, Austin Rover knew it was on to a good thing with its special editions, and the Ritz was the first of a string of Mini specials with London high-life connotations, arriving in January 1985.

The Ritz set the tone for almost all future special editions by basing itself on the City E. Its exterior embellishments consisted of a metallic Silver Leaf paint scheme with red taping along the body and on the boot, bright 'Ritz' motifs, and colour-keyed Nimbus Grey grille, wheelarch spats, drip rail and door mirror. It had a standard locking fuel filler cap and 12in alloy wheels (usually optional for the Mayfair). There was a chrome finish for the bumpers, door handles, boot handle and exhaust tailpipe.

The interior was fully colour co-ordinated with Claret Red/Prussian Blue/Osprey Grey velvet-

panelled seat facings plus matching backs and head restraints. The whole interior was rigorously colour-keyed, with matching Prussian Blue facia, front and rear seat belts, carpets and door bins. There were Ritz logos on the seat backs and the centre of the steering wheel. Standard equipment included door bins, rear seat belts, a three-spoke steering wheel, Mayfair double instrument pack and radio. The cost was £3,798, with 2,000 being earmarked for the UK market and a further 1,725 for export.

Mini Chelsea (1986)

Once sold out of the Ritz, Austin Rover had another go with the Chelsea, again based on the City E and announced in January 1986. Production began in the same month that the 5 millionth Mini rolled off the production line in February 1986.

It was startlingly painted in Targa Red with red and silver twin coachlines, plus 'The Chelsea' logos painted on the rear flanks and bootlid. There were alloy wheels, low-profile tyres and opening rear windows once again.

Inside, there was Osprey Grey fabric upholstery with 'The Chelsea' script in red on the reclining seat backrests and red piping in the seats, head restraints and door casings. The facia and door handles were finished in black and the triple

The Chelsea boasted standard alloy wheels, twin door mirrors and opening rear quarter-windows. The paint scheme was bold red with silver-and-red coachlines. Inside, there was the three-instrument binnacle which by then was standard on the Mayfair.

instrument pack contained a rev-counter, while the steering wheel was described in promotional material as 'soft feel'.

At a price of £3,898 – the most expensive Mini to date – the Chelsea was built in quite a large production run, although Britain had only 1,500 examples.

The Chelsea

Externally, the Piccadilly looked rather like an ordinary Mayfair except that it was painted gold and had chrome bumpers and door handles. The interior was predominantly brown and had few luxury items, making the Piccadilly one of the least exciting of all Mini special editions.

Mini Piccadilly (1986)

The Chelsea sold out so rapidly that the Piccadilly followed only a matter of months later, in May 1986. Once again, the transformation of the City E base model consisted almost entirely of cosmetic twiddlings.

The paint finish this time was Cashmere Gold with a coachline bearing a 'Piccadilly' motif, which also appeared on the boot. Instead of alloy wheels, there were full-sized plastic wheeltrims, but the door handles and bumpers were chrome-plated and the rear windows hinged open.

The interior was trimmed in Bitter Chocolate,

Coffee and Claret velvet with a 'Piccadilly' motif in each reclining front seat. There were standard head restraints, a push-button radio and a three-spoke steering wheel. The cost: £3,928. Total number built: 2,500, with many going to France and Japan.

Mini Park Lane (1987)

The last of the 'Upper Class London' special editions was the Park Lane announced in January 1987. Once again, this was based on the City E.

All-black paintwork with bright grille surround, bumpers and door handles distinguished the Park Lane, which had special striping and identifying decals, as ever. There were full wheeltrims, black wheelarch spats and sill finishers, a lockable filler cap and tinted windows, the rear ones hinged.

The interior came in beige and dark velvet, included head restraints and the inevitable 'Park Lane' logo in the front seat backrests. A stereo radio/cassette was offered as standard in the price of £4,194 and 1,500 were intended for sale in the UK, the total build reaching 4,000. Japan took some 700 Park Lanes.

In contrast with the Piccadilly, no-one could mistake the Mini Park Lane. It was all-black, with bold white-and-red decals on the sides and boot and chrome bumpers, grille surround and handles. It also had tinted windows.

The Park Lane interior was also much more jazzy. The seats were upholstered in beige and black velvet with the 'Park Lane' logo incorporated into the front seat backs.

1987 was a year of all-white special editions. The Mini Advantage was one of the best, with a consistent tennis theme running throughout. The body sides were painted with what looked like a tennis net and ball, a theme which continued inside the car.

Mini Advantage (1987)

To take 'advantage' of the tennis season, the Mini Advantage was launched first in France in May 1987 to coincide with the French Open. It appeared in Britain one month later to catch Wimbledon. Indeed, it was originally to be called the Mini Wimbledon, but the Queen's Club vetoed the idea.

Once more based on the City E, the bodywork was in Diamond White with matching wheel-trims. The lower body sides were decked out with a sort of tennis net finish, with a bold 'Advantage' logo and tennis ball scrawled across them. There was also a passenger's side door mirror, tinted glass and hinged rear quarter-windows.

The tennis net theme continued inside the Advantage, with Flint Grey-and-Jade Green criss-cross cloth upholstery and little green tennis balls on the front seats. The triple-instrument binnacle came from the Mayfair.

The Advantage cost £4,286 and, of the 4,675 produced, only 2,500 were set aside for Britain. In Germany, the model was known by the name Mini Masters, with corresponding side decals.

Mini Red Hot and Mini Jet Black (1988)

Mini limited editions now entered a phase of frippery, perhaps a nostalgic nod to the Sixties, with a pair of 'fun' Minis simultaneously launched at the Brussels Motor Show in January 1988. They arrived in Britain in February. Their basis, as usual, was the Mini City.

The Red Hot was painted red and the Jet Black, unsurprisingly, was black. Both acquired silver wheeltrims and chrome bumpers, door handles and tailpipe. They had identifying badges on their grilles and similar decals on their flanks and boots. Both models had special red-lined wheel-trims. Opening rear quarter-lights were standard.

Interiors were described as 'sporty', decked out with black velour seats with red piping, and the familiar 'Red Hot' or 'Jet Black' insignia on the seats. The carpets, facia and three-spoke steering wheel were all black. Standard equipment included tinted glass and, in the UK, a pushbutton radio.

A total of 2,000 were made for the UK at a price of £4,382, but a further 4,000 were built for export to various European countries, plus Japan and Taiwan, making them probably the most popular of all Mini special editions.

Probably the most numerous Mini special editions were the Red Hot and Jet Black, totalling 6000. The Red Hot was painted in a very bright red colour with contrasting black coachline and decals.

The Jet Black was painted black with contrasting red coachline and decals. On both editions, there was a silver finish for the wheel-trims, bumpers, handles and tailpipe and both had an additional identifying badge in their grille.

The Mini Designer of 1988 was available in either white or black with contrasting coachlines and colour-keyed grey exterior trim. Echoing its origins as a Mary Quant special edition, it had a Quant daisy motif where the Mini badge would normally be on the bonnet.

Mini Designer (1988)

The Mini Designer, a name with more than a reflection of late Eighties values, was launched in June 1988, available in two colours, Black or Diamond White, with Nimbus Grey headlamp surrounds, bumpers, door handles, spats and grille. Twin coachlines – white on black cars and black on white cars – ended with a 'Designer' logo, which also appeared on the boot. On the bonnet there was a Mary Quant daisy badge. The special edition was to have been named after her, but the marketing men thought 'Designer' was safer.

The interiors of both black and white editions were identical: striking black-and-white striped fabric with red piping, echoing a Sixties Mary Quant theme: she endorsed the interior decor herself and her signature appeared on the front seat squabs. There was also red piping on the doors and red seat belts. It came with a DC 330 stereo radio/cassette, leather-bound steering wheel – with the Mary Quant daisy motif – and two vanity mirrors. Tinted glass was standard, as were hinged rear windows. Total cost was £4,654, and 2,000 were built for UK consumption.

Mary Quant in the Mini Designer: the bold black-and-white striped seats echoed a design theme of hers, and she endorsed the special edition, her signature appearing on labels stitched into the front seats. The leatherbound steering wheel also had a Mary Quant daisy in its centre.

Mini Racing, Mini Flame, Mini Rose and Mini Sky (1989)

This clutch of Mini special editions presaged the huge celebrations of the Mini's 30th birthday in 1989. They were launched simultaneously in January 1989, with the Racing and Flame harking back to the Mini-Cooper, while the Sky and Rose flaunted pure fashion – although the differences between the four were hardly great.

The Racing and Flame were basically identical apart from their paint schemes – British Racing Green for the former and Flame Red for the latter – plus different decals on the rear haunches. Each had a Cooper-style white roof.

The Sky and Rose were also very alike, but the former came in white with a pastel blue roof, the latter with a pastel pink roof. All four special editions had white full-width wheeltrims.

There were new interior trim fabrics – colour-coded pink and blue Crayon fabric in the Rose and Sky – and a standard stereo radio/cassette. The Racing and Flame cost £4,795, the Sky and Rose £4,695, the extra premium for the former

pair being accounted for by their standard fitment of a sports steering wheel and rev-counter. These four editions were built until August 1989; the Flame and Racing sold 2,000 examples, while the Sky and Rose notched up only 1,000.

Four editions in one stroke: the 1989 Flame, Rose, Sky and Racing. The front pair were Cooperesque in appeal, while the rear pair were more effete, with their pastel-coloured roofs. All had the new Mayfair-style wheeltrims in bold white.

Mini Thirty (1989)

This was the true Mini birthday model, advertised by Rover as "The new 30th anniversary Special Edition". The Thirty was a smart-looking special which sold very well and was used as the basis of the forthcoming Mini-Cooper. It was launched in June 1989 and was based on the Mayfair model.

Two paint schemes were on offer: pearlescent Cherry Red or Black, both with duo-tone coachlines (black-and-white on red cars and red-and-grey on black cars). Both finishes boasted an extra coat of clear lacquer. There were commemorative '1959-1989' crests on the flanks and a similar new badge for the bonnet. The grille returned to the old chrome look, as did the bumpers, door and boot handles. The wheelarch spats, door mirrors and sill finishers were all colour-matched with the main body colour. They also had very fetching eight-spoke Minilite-style alloy wheels as standard, soon to become a standard feature on the Mini-Cooper.

Inside, the seats were trimmed in Lightning cloth and faced with black leather. The red leather steering wheel was matched by red trim piping and Cherry Red cut pile carpet. The '1959–1989' crest appeared on both the front seats and steering wheel. The door casings matched the seat trim, there were coloured carpets, new gear-lever gaiter and knob, new handbrake grip and a standard R570 security-coded stereo/radio cassette. Each buyer of the Mini Thirty also received a leather-bound Mini book.

Of the 3,000 cars built for Britain, 2,000 were

The Mini Thirty was a fine birthday present for the Mini and easily the best-equipped version yet made. Available in black or red – each with a deeper lacquered finish – the Thirty looked very dashing with its Minilite-replica alloy wheels, chrome-effect grille, body-coloured trim and anniversary crests on the bonnet and body sides.

in red and 1,000 in black. The cost was £5,599 for the manual version, of which 2,800 were built for UK consumption. There was also an automatic version – the first automatic Mini special edition – of which only 200 were available in the UK.

Mini Racing Green, Mini Flame Red and Mini Check Mate (1990)

Flushed with the success of the previous year's anniversary specials, the Racing and Flame names were revived for another spin alongside a new name, Check Mate, in February 1990.

The only features to distinguish the models

Three sports-style special editions for 1990: the Flame, Checkmate and Racing. In contrast with the previous year's Flame and Racing editions, this trio sported spoked alloy wheels and came with the original 1961 Cooper 3.44:1 final drive. Strangely for an edition with sporting undertones, automatic transmission was offered as an extra.

from each other were their paint schemes and appropriate decals: the Racing came in British Racing Green with a white roof, the Flame was red with a white roof and the Check Mate was black with a white roof. With their Minilite-style alloy wheels, their similarity with the old Mini-Cooper was readily apparent. The Mini's racing heritage was alluded to by a bonnet-mounted crossed-flag badge. Chrome bumpers were standard.

The Cooper allusion extended to the fitment of the old Cooper 'S' 3.44:1 final-drive ratio. Any of the three limited editions could be bought with the new Rover-approved John Cooper Performance Kit (detailed in *SECTION FOUR*), effectively creating a 'new' Mini-Cooper. (Rover launched its own Mini-Cooper within a matter of months – see below.)

Interiors were fitted with Black Crayon seat trim and red-piped door trim, and included the three-instrument binnacle and an R361 three-band stereo radio/cassette.

Apart from its door-mounted graphic, the Studio 2 was not an exceptional special edition. It had a chrome-effect grille and came in a choice of three colours (black, blue or grey).

Automatic transmission could be specified as an option at £895. Each of these special editions cost £5,455, and 2,500 were made for British customers, with many more exported.

Mini Studio 2 (1990)

In June 1990 came the new Studio 2 special edition. This was a name previously used for Metro special editions in 1987 and 1988 and the graphic imagery of those cars was transferred to the Mini Studio 2, which again was based on the City model.

It followed familiar practice, with 'Studio 2' decals on the front doors, bootlid and seat facings, while a chrome grille and full wheeltrims were standard. There were three paint schemes: Black, Nordic Blue or Storm Grey, each with a City-style green stripe and three green dots just below the window line.

Inside the colour-keyed cabin, there were unique Doeskin seat covers incorporating a green diagonal stripe and, on the front seats, an embossed 'Studio 2' panel. The three-spoke steering wheel had a unique green 'Mini' badge on it. Opening rear quarter-lights and an R750 security-coded stereo were standard.

The cost was £5,375 and 2,000 were built for Britain.

The special introductory edition of the Nineties Mini-Cooper looked just right and, at last, featured a 1,275cc engine. With its Minilite-style wheels, chrome-effect grille, body-coloured door mirrors and wheelarch extensions, Cooper winged bonnet badge, Mini-Cooper laurel garland decals, evocative white bonnet stripes carrying John Cooper's signature and front driving lamps, it was bound to be a big success.

Mini-Cooper (1990)

Before it became a regular production model in September 1990, Rover built a Special Products-developed limited edition of just 1,000 Mini-Coopers from July. The new model predictably caused a huge stir and the car sold out before it even had a chance to reach the showrooms. As a consequence, these have become highly cherished models.

The interior of the special-edition Mini-Cooper featured black leather seat inserts, red piping in the seats, doors and rear-quarter casings, red carpets and a red leather-bound steering wheel.

The new Mini-Cooper was based on the specification of the successful Mini Thirty, but differed mechanically, being the first Mini for 10 years to be fitted with the 1,275cc engine: this was a 61bhp version of the old 1,275cc MG Metro engine, with catalyst, revised final drive and so on: for the car's mechanical details, refer to *SECTION FOUR*.

The special edition differed from the production version in that it came with standard white bonnet stripes bearing the John Cooper signature, had body-coloured door mirrors and wheelarches, a sunroof, black leather trim, red carpets and a red leather steering wheel.

Body colours were British Racing Green, red or black, all with white roofs (the same schemes as the 1989 Racing, Flame and Check Mate editions).

There was very little that was exceptional about the Mini Neon of 1991. It was based on the City and added May-fair wheeltrims, opening rear quarter-lights, twin door mirrors, colour-keyed front seat belts, pink-and-white coachlines and 'Neon' motifs on the body sides and steering wheel.

There were, of course, special new 'Cooper' badges. Standard equipment included a glass sunroof, tinted glass, auxiliary driving lamps, chrome grille and alloy wheels.

The 1,000 cars made available in the UK were all quickly snapped up at a price of £6,995. A further 650 commemorative Coopers were made for Japan.

Mini Neon (1991)

The Neon was another style-orientated limited edition based on the City, launched in February 1991. More basic than most special editions, it was also quite a restrained effort.

The body colour was Nordic Blue metallic and there were chrome bumpers, door handles, grille and exhaust tailpipe. Twin coachlines extended back to a logo which read 'Neon by Mini' (!). There were full-width wheeltrims and a standard passenger's side door mirror.

The interior was quite understated: it was trimmed in Chevron velour, with a 'Neon' badge on the steering wheel and included an R280 digital stereo radio/cassette as standard. As ever, it had hinged rear windows.

The price was £5,570, and some 1,500 Neons were made.

The limited edition Mini Cabriolet was basically a Mini-Cooper converted in Germany to Rover's order. In contrast with the later Rover-built Cabriolet, it had a hood frame hinged at the B-post – therefore no glass rear windows – and a very wide bodykit. Just visible are the small identifying 'LAMM Design' decals on the doors.

Mini Cabriolet (1991)

Like the Mini-Cooper, the Mini Cabriolet was first offered as a special edition, appearing in June 1991. In fact, it was a German conversion which gained Rover's seal of approval to be sold through

Rover dealerships. The Cabriolet was based on the Mini-Cooper's mechanical specification, but had drastically altered bodywork, effected in Germany by LAMM Autohaus, the German Rover dealer.

The main change was to the roof, which was chopped off and replaced by a folding fabric hood. The rear windows were replaced by clear plastic incorporated into the rather tent-like hood. Substantial strengthening was added in the body-shell, mainly by enhancing the sill sections and adding a new crossmember. There was also a full colour-matched bodykit, featuring a massive front spoiler, extended wheelarches, side skirts and integral bumpers. Huge 175/50 tyres were fitted on five-spoke Revolution alloy wheels. As if the changes could not be spotted, there was a small 'Cabriolet' badge on the boot and small 'LAMM Design' decals on the doors. Only one colour was available: pearlescent Cherry Red, with a matching maroon hood.

Inside, there was a wood-grain dashboard containing three instruments and wooden door cappings and gear knob. The seats and trim came from the Mayfair, and there was a Cooper-style leather steering wheel and removable Clarion

The interior of the Cabriolet was certainly plush, with its full-width walnut facia – containing three dials – wooden door cappings, gear knob and door pulls, Clarion stereo and leather-bound steering wheel. The seats, however, were mere Mayfair items.

With its hood erected, the LAMM-built Cabriolet looked somewhat like a pram. The side and rear windows were made of flexible Perspex.

CRH50 stereo unit.

At a huge cost of £12,250, only 75 were made available through just 12 selected Rover dealers in Britain in 1991. Yet the model sold out immediately, inspiring Rover to launch a regular production Cabriolet, in modified form, the following year (see *SECTION FOUR*). LAMM continued to offer the Cabriolet conversion in Germany, which is still available at the time of writing.

The electrically-controlled full-length folding sunroof of the British Open Classic made it one of the most desirable Minis. It was an attractive-looking edition, too, with alloy wheels, chrome-type grille, body-colour door mirrors and number-plate shroud and chrome trim. The interior was sumptuously decked out in tweed and leather.

Mini British Open Classic (1992)

Rover returned to the tennis theme with this June 1992-launched limited edition, which it strangely referred to as the Mini British Open, despite the fact that all the logos read 'British Open Classic'.

There was a bit of word-play with this limited edition as a folding sunroof appeared for the first time on a British Mini (Minis exported to Japan had had this option for some time). This was also the first special edition to be based on the new 1.3-litre Mini.

The main feature of the British Open Classic was the electrically-operated full-length folding fabric sunroof with a wind deflector fitted at its leading edge. The only colour available was metallic British Racing Green. The 'British Open Classic' logo bore an ever-so-English coat-of-arms which appeared on the rear flanks and boot. Minilite-type alloy wheels were standard, as were chrome bumpers and handles, a chrome-effect grille and hinged rear quarter-lights.

Inside, there was Countryman Tweed upholstery in Stone Beige with leather inserts and contrasting piping on the seats. The steering wheel came leather-bound and a little 'By Appointment to Her Majesty the Queen' label was stitched into the front seats. An R552 stereo system was standard.

An example of this unusual special edition could be bought for a stately £7,195 and 1,000 were earmarked for the British market, with export markets also targeted.

The Italian Job was an example of life mimicking art, as the cars harked back to the film of the same name in which Mini-Coopers were seen trouncing Turin. It was basically a budget attempt to look a bit like a Cooper, but it had an ordinary grille painted white, black bumpers and wheelarch spats, black-and-white bonnet stripes and white spoked alloy wheels. Colours available were red, white, blue and green.

Mini Italian Job (1992)

This special edition exploited the prominent role played by Mini-Coopers in the 1969 film, *The Italian Job*, starring Michael Caine and Noel Cowerd. Several charity runs to Italy and back were organized, backed by the original cast members. The Italian Job special edition was launched in October 1992.

It tried to mimic the style of the Mini-Coopers as seen in the film, basically offering a car which looked rather like the new-generation Cooper, but it did not go like it (having just the 50bhp 1,275cc engine). So there were bonnet stripes and twin driving lamps. Four colours were offered: Flame

Red, Diamond White, metallic British Racing Green and, for the first time, a rather odd-looking colour called Electric Blue, each with colour co-ordinated twin wing mirrors. There was also a contrasting roof colour, novel white grille, white wheels, black bumpers, tinted glass, crossed Italian/British flag decals on the flanks and boot and a special 'Italian Job' badge on the bonnet.

Inside, the trim was Black Tweed and there was a three-spoke steering wheel incorporating the 'Italian Job' badge. There was also the Mayfair triple instrument pack and opening rear quarter-windows. The cost was £5,995 and 1,750 were made, 1,000 for Britain and 750 for Italy.

Mini Rio (1993)

The Mini Rio was described by Rover as "exclusive and fashionable", but then weren't they all? Again it was based on the Mini Sprite and was launched in June 1993.

There was a choice of three colours: Black, pearlescent Caribbean Blue or metallic Polynesian Turquoise – colours which could normally be specified only as extra-cost options on the standard Mini. The usual decal treatment for the flanks and boot consisted of a 'Rio' motif with colourful streamers.

The 1993 Mini Rio was another simple but effective sprucing of the basic Mini Sprite. Just about the only distinctive features were its graphics, its bright interior trim and its availability in unusual colours: black, metallic blue or metallic turquoise.

Inside, the trim was black with bright green Spira panels on the doors and seats. An R652 stereo radio/cassette was standard.

The cost was £5,495 and the 750 units built were sold only in the UK – making the Rio one of the rarest Mini special editions.

Taking its name from the colour in which it was painted (Tahiti Blue), the Mini Tahiti was quite basic in specification, but it did boast spoked alloy wheels, chrome bumpers and twin door mirrors. With only 500 made, it was a rare Mini special edition.

Mini Tahiti (1993)

The second Mini special edition of 1993 was the Tahiti. Introduced in October 1993, it was based on the Mini Sprite.

The paintwork was pearlescent Tahiti Blue – a colour previously reserved for the Rover 200 Coupe only – with 'Tahiti' decals – complete with silhouetted palm trees – placed on the flanks and bootlid. Cooper-type alloy wheels were standard, as were chrome bumpers. Yet costs were kept low in the Tahiti by doing without hinged rear quarters – almost a first for a special edition! – and sticking quite closely to the Sprite specification.

Inside, there was black trim with blue-and-black Hatchings door and seat inserts, plus colour-keyed seat belts. An R652 radio/cassette with twin speakers was included in the price of £5,795 for the manual version and £6,715 for the automatic. The Tahiti was reserved strictly for the UK and was made in a limited run of just 500 – excluding the Cabriolet, the rarest Mini special edition of all, which is a shame as it was such an unexceptional variant.

The Mini-Cooper Monte Carlo was not strictly a special edition, merely a limited-availability option pack for the Mini-Cooper. Rover called it a "dealer showroom Monte Carlo Rally Anniversary Decal Kit" and it consisted of an extra pair of spotlamps, white racing patches and a set of 'Monte Carlo Rally' stickers for the body.

Mini-Cooper Monte Carlo (January 1994)

In celebration of the 30th anniversary of Paddy Hopkirk's historic win in the 1964 Monte Carlo Rally, Rover launched a Monte Carlo 'rally anniversary decal kit' for the Mini-Cooper in January 1994, available through dealers as an option when a Mini-Cooper was bought. This was altogether more ambitious than the dealer-fitted options pack of the same name which was offered in 1991.

It was essentially a cosmetic exercise to make

the Cooper look like a rally-spec car, consisting of an extra pair of spotlamps – to make four in total – white racing number patches on the doors, John Cooper's signature on the front wings, Cooper wheel centres, a single white coachline and special stickers mimicking the Monte Carlo Rally plates on the bonnet, boot and body sides: they read '1964-1994 Rallye Monte Carlo', with a Mini-Cooper laurel garland.

The package was offered as a limited edition accessory kit rather than a true limited edition. Amazingly, Rover charged no extra for the goodies if the car was bought new: £7,195 was the same price as that for the standard Mini-Cooper.

Mini 35 (1994)

In celebration of the 35th anniversary of the Mini, Rover launched the Mini 35 in June 1994. As usual, it was based on the Sprite. Yet this was not the glory-bird which previous anniversary editions had been. Its specification was pared down to a price rather than up to a quality. There was a choice of three exterior colours, two of them new for the '35': pearlescent Nevada Red, metallic Arizona Blue and the familiar White Diamond. All sported a silver coachline.

Identifying decals on the flanks were complemented by special badges for the bonnet and steering wheel boss. There was also a chrome grille, lock set and door handles, plus opening rear windows.

The fairly basic interior was upholstered in a trendy blue-and-pink cloth trim called Jamboree, while the seats additionally had black PVC backs and sides and black doeskin fabric side rolls. An R652 stereo was standard. Spoked alloy wheels and automatic transmission were options.

The price was a very reasonable £5,695 and 1,000 were made for the British market. Other markets like France, Italy and Japan were offered their own unique versions with different names.

The 35th anniversary Mini was rather unadventurous. Here an example poses with Mini Number One.

Inside, the Mini 35 looked very much like a Sprite, but with the addition of bright new trim.

Mini-Cooper
Monte Carlo (July 1994)

While the options pack launched in January 1994 celebrated the 30th anniversary of Paddy Hopkirk's victory in the Monte Carlo Rally, the official special edition Monte Carlo commemorated Hopkirk's return to the rally in 1994 (which he completed with co-driver Ron Crellin). The Monte Carlo was launched in July 1994.

Based on the Mini-Cooper 1.3i, the Monte Carlo featured a distinctive new exterior treatment, with Gunmetal-finished alloy wheels fitted with wider 165/60 R12 tyres and 'Cooper' centre badges. There were two extra foglamps on the front and a decal scheme which read '1964–1967 Rallye Monte Carlo'. Two paint schemes were offered: Black or Flame Red, the latter with body-coloured wheelarch extensions.

Inside, red vinyl seats with cream cloth centre panels reflected the Sixties Cooper interior. There were also red seat belts, red carpets, red leather steering wheel and red leather gear knob and gaiter. The instruments had cream faces, set in a Mayfair-style full-width wood facia.

The Monte-Carlo cost £7,995 and a strictly limited run of just 200 cars was envisaged.

The luxurious mainly red-and-cream interior of the Mini-Cooper Monte Carlo, with one of the cream-faced main instruments visible ahead of the leather-covered three-spoke steering wheel.

Rover's official Monte Carlo limited edition was easily identified by its gunmetal alloy wheels and special decals. Only 200 were to be built.

SECTION SIX

Commercial Minis

The extremely versatile layout of the Mini's drivetrain allowed an almost limitless variety of other bodies to be fitted. BMC leapt straight in with its first official bodywork variation with the Mini Van only five months after the launch of the saloon Mini. This was a studied move to capitalize on the substantial market for small commercial vehicles which the Mini soon began to take by storm.

The ¼-ton van was based on a Mini floorpan with its wheelbase extended by 4 inches to just over 7 feet. The bodyshell was heavily modified aft of the B-pillar to become a proper van, with its roofline continuing the line begun by the saloon. Together with its increased rear overhang, the total length of the Minivan grew by 9.5in to 129.875in.

Access to the functional load area was via twin side-mounted rear doors. As previously explained in respect of the estate versions of the Mini, the only reason why BMC adopted these rather than the cheaper alternative of a single rear door was that with twin doors each van took up less space on the production line (they were assembled with

their doors open). Certainly there were no practical advantages to the double-door system.

Some extra enhancement was necessary to maintain the body rigidity lost by the omission of the saloon's rear bulkhead. The flat floor was swaged and boxed over by a raised load platform. Under this, directly behind the seats, were stowed the spare wheel (on the nearside) and the battery (on the offside) with a new 6-gallon oblong fuel tank slotted in behind the rear axle line.

The new van offered many attractions to the commercial user: its load height was a mere 17.5in from the ground and the total usable volume was some 46cu ft (or 58cu ft if the passenger's seat was removed). The load platform was a useful 55in long and 53.75in wide, and the nominal load capacity of the van was given as 5cwt.

The only real technical change was to the rear suspension, which had longer turrets, increasing ride height at the rear end. The suspension was stiffer to accept the greater loads the van would be expected to carry, although its weight remained almost the same as the saloon, thanks to a stripped-out interior.

Cost-cutting measures for the Mini Van included a stamped-out front grille – as opposed to the separate grilles fitted to the saloons – and rear quarter-bumpers in place of a full-width bumper. The fuel filler was sited in a recess on the offside rear wing. Twin wing mirrors were required by law for commercial vehicles, but an interior mirror was not, so that was omitted from the standard specification! Trim was kept to a bare minimum, with expanses of bare painted metal

The Van version of the Mini was based on a lengthened floorpan. It was the most basic Mini variant, with a unique stamped-out grille (the same for Austin and Morris variants). Note the wing-mounted mirrors, the absence of an interior mirror and fitment of an Austin A35 van roof vent. (BMIHT)

An admirable load volume could be reached through double rear doors. The load area was strengthened with a second steel floor, under which were fitted the fuel tank, spare wheel and battery. (BMIHT)

The BMC photographer has tried desperately to make the optional rear seat conversion for the Van look comfortable and spacious. It was not! Note how the raised floor has been chopped away for legroom, necessitating the relocation of the battery (left) and spare wheel.

and a heavy-duty floor covering in the interior. As a result, the price was kept down to £360 – with no purchase tax being payable – compared with the basic saloon's price of £497 – of which a hefty percentage was purchase tax. Both Austin and Morris versions were offered.

Within a very short time, BMC marketed a conversion kit to turn the van into a four-seater for the princely sum of £15. This was attractive to many private customers as a cheap route to owning a new four-seater car: as the van was classed as a commercial vehicle, paying purchase tax could be avoided (the presence of rear windows was the deciding factor in whether to classify a vehicle as a van or passenger car). For the conversion, the load platform had to be shortened to provide a rear footwell. The battery and spare wheel both had to be moved as a result, the spare being bolted and strapped to the body side in front of the wheelarch, and the battery now sitting in a fibre box on the offside. A folding rear bench seat was provided for two rear passengers. As well as the BMC conversion, there were plenty of other aftermarket four-seater kits.

The obvious disadvantages of a four-seater van over a saloon were the extremely basic specification and lack of visibility, while the law also restricted the top speed of such vehicles to a paltry 40mph on pain of paying a hefty fine. Such was the cost of economy motoring.

The van was used as the basis for the Mini estate derivatives launched later in 1960 (see *SECTION ONE*). The Mini Pick-up followed in

January 1961. This was essentially the same as the Mini Van, but had cutaway upper rear body sides and rear roof section. A bulkhead with a full-width flat screen was fitted behind the seats to restore lost rigidity and there was a drop-down tailgate secured by hinged metal bars. There was also a hinged rear number-plate *a la* saloon, which was useful when carrying loads longer than the length of the floor. This also meant that a full-width chrome rear bumper could be fitted in place of the quarter-bumpers of the van, although later Pick-ups also had simple quarter-bumpers. The Pick-up also acquired unique rear light clusters to suit its rear panels.

The distance between the load floor and the lapped and gusseted top of the Pick-up's rear body sides was 17.25in. This could be improved by fitting the canvas tilt onto its detachable metal tube frame, increasing the enclosed space to almost as much as the van (the roofline being only 0.25in lower at 37in). The load volume to waist level was a useful 26.75cu ft.

The standard engine for both commercial Minis was the 848cc A-series, but the 998cc engine was offered as an option from 1967, in which case the 3.44:1 final drive was supplied instead of the usual 3.76:1.

All long-wheelbase Minis were rubber-sprung and never received the Hydrolastic suspension of the saloon. In fact, the Mini Van and Pick-up remained firmly rooted in the past as the passenger cars forged ahead with ever-more sophisticated specifications: external door hinges, old-style rear lights, sliding windows and 1959-style door bins remained on these commercial Minis right until the end.

Yet there were some changes over the years. The remote gearchange and most of the mechanical improvements were adopted for the commercials, except in the suspension department, which remained the rubber cone system. Some of the interior refinements of the saloon also went into the commercial versions, including the improved switchgear and column-mounted stalks. An interior mirror and door-mounted exterior mirrors became standard for the last few years.

Both versions were strong sellers, particularly the Mini Van, which saw service with many British institutions like the AA, RAC, Police and Post Office, as well as thousands of businesses large and small.

Towards the end of their respective lives, the Van was more commonly sold with the 998cc engine and the 848cc Pick-up bowed out in 1980. The last Vans and Pick-ups were sold in 1983, by which time they were only available to fleet order. Well over half a million commercial Minis had been made.

The Mini Moke is worth a brief mention here because it was officially sold as one of the ¼-ton Mini commercial range from 1964–68. The Moke's story is told in full in *SECTION EIGHT*.

Austin Se7en Van (1960–61), Austin Minivan (1962–69), Morris Minivan (1960–69) and Mini Van (1969–83)

The first commercial Mini was the van and it was built from January 1960. With its lengthened wheelbase and capacious enclosed rear load space, it was a practical and economical van in the smallest class, with a surprising ability to consume goods. Entry to the load area was via twin side-hinging doors with separate windows.

For the first nine years, the van came in both Austin and Morris versions, although the differences between the two were confined to badging. They were more basic in trim than the saloon.

Although it was rebadged as a Mini like all the other Mini variants in 1969, the Van retained the old MkI body style, including its grille, sliding windows, external door hinges and so on.

Vans could be bought purely and simply for use by small businesses or BMC would build them to suit specialized requirements if a fleet was ordered. For example, the Post Office ordered mail vans with special latches, partitioning, mail boxes and so on. Perhaps the most famous user of Mini vans was the AA, which ran a huge fleet as patrol transport, the vehicles being painted in the familiar yellow livery with roof-mounted identifying plaques.

Changes were few. The 1-litre engine was offered from 1967, but would never be as popular as the 850 version. A front passenger's seat, originally available only as an optional extra, eventually became standard.

Austin and Morris badging disappeared in 1969 and the model was renamed simply Mini Van. Both 850 and 1000 versions were offered until the model's demise in 1983, when it was effectively replaced by the Metro Van.

Specification

	Van 850	Van 1000
Engine	848cc 4-cyl OHV	998cc 4-cyl OHV
Engine designation	8MB	9WR, 99H
Bore/stroke	62.94 x 68.26mm	64.59 x 76.2mm
Compression ratio	8.3:1	8.3:1
Power output	33bhp at 5,300rpm	38bhp at 5,250rpm
	33bhp at 5,300rpm (from 1974)	39bhp at 4,750rpm (from 1974)
Torque	44lb.ft at 2,900rpm	52lb.ft at 2,700rpm
	40lb.ft at 2,500rpm (from 1974)	51.5lb.ft at 2,000rpm (from 1974)
Transmission	Four-speed manual: Ratios: 4th 3.765, 3rd 5.317, 2nd 8.176, 1st 13.657, Rev 13.657.	4th 3.44, 3rd 4.86, 2nd 7.47 1st 12.48.
Steering	Rack & pinion	
Brakes	Hydraulic drum/drum	
Suspension	Independent	
	Front: Wishbones, rubber cones, Armstrong telescopic dampers	
	Rear: Trailing arms, rubber cones, Armstrong telescopic dampers	
Wheels	Pressed steel 3.5 x 10in	
Tyres	5.20 x 10in Dunlop C41 cross-ply, radial-ply from 1976	
Wheelbase	84.25in (2,138mm)	
Length	129.875in (3,299mm)	
Width	55.5in (1,410mm)	
Height	54.5in (1,384mm)	
Front track	47.75in (1,213mm)	
Rear track	45.875in (1,165mm)	
Weight	1,371lb (622kg)	
Fuel tank	6gal (27l)	
Load capacity	46cu ft (1.3cu m) or 58cu ft (1.64cu m) with passenger seat removed	

Performance

Maximum speed	75mph (121km/h)	
0–60mph		30sec
Average fuel consumption		40mpg

Optional extras

Front passenger seat
Rear seat conversion kit
PVC floor covering
Windscreen washer (until 1962)
Seat belts (until 1976)

Interior rear-view mirror
998cc engine with 3.44:1 final drive (from 1967)
'L' pack for Mini Van 850 (from 1979)

Range

Austin Se7en Van (1960–61)
Austin Minivan (1962–69)
Morris Minivan (1960–69)
Mini Van 850 (1969–83)
Mini Van 1000 (1969–79)
Mini Van 1000L (1979–83)

Production history

January 1960: Austin Se7en Van and Morris Minivan first produced (Chassis Number AAV7 12101 – Austin, and MAV4 12601 – Morris). Cost: £360.

January 1962: Austin version now known as Minivan.

October 1962: Baulk-ring synchromesh progressively introduced (Engine Number 405271 – Austin, and 412992 – Morris). Windscreen washers, interior light and bumper overriders standard.

October 1967: 998cc engine option introduced (with 3.44:1 final drive).

October 1969: Marque name changed to Mini, and van rebadged Mini Van. Negative-earth electrics, mechanical fuel pump.

October 1970: Ignition shield introduced.

February 1972: Improved synchromesh fitted.

April 1972: Split needle-roller bearings on idler gears.

December 1972: Improved driveshaft boots and alternator standard.

April 1973: Rod-operated gearchange introduced.

June 1973: Plunging CV joints on inboard end of new driveshafts.

May 1974: HS4 swing-needle carburettor and revised manifold, air cleaner and exhaust manifold fitted. Ignition timing altered.

June 1974: Twin-silencer exhaust fitted.

October 1975: 88° thermostat standard.

May 1976: Twin column-mounted control stalks fitted, new rocker-switch type panel incorporating hazard lights standard, larger pedals from Allegro, ignition/steering lock from BL Princess fitted.

July 1977: Padded steering wheel and handbrake grip from Austin Allegro fitted.

December 1978: New 'Mini 95' badging, indicating gross weight.

November 1979: 'L' pack introduced as standard on Mini Van 1000 and optional on 850: cloth-faced seats, carpet, passenger's sun visor and additional sound deadening.

May 1983: Mini Van discontinued.

Total production: Austin/Morris Minivan 344,249 (of which approx 174,500 Austin and approx 169,250 Morris); Mini Van 850: 94,899; Mini Van 1000: 82,356. Total: 521,494.

Austin Se7en Pick-up (1961), Austin Mini Pick-up (1961–69), Morris Mini Pick-up (1961–69) and Mini Pick-up (1969–83)

Twelve months after the arrival of the Van came the Pick-up. This shared the same floorpan and mechanical specification, but had different bodywork aft of the B-posts, with a closed-in cab and open Pick-up rear tray. Access to the load area was by a drop-down tailgate.

The Pick-up was initially available in Austin and Morris versions with minimal differences between them. A canvas tilt could be fitted sus-

The Pick-up was essentially the same as the Van below the waist, except for the addition of a solid rear bulkhead and a drop-down tailgate. With its canvas tilt erected over twin steel tube hoops, the Pick-up almost became a van again. The roll-up rear screen incorporated a transparent plastic 'window'. Note the unique Pick-up rear lights.

pended on a tubular metal frame, which attached at the front end and into the rear body sides. This weather-sealed the load area. Initially, the tilt was offered only as an optional extra, but it eventually became a standard feature.

From 1967, there was the option of a 998cc engine, which became the only choice as of 1980, when the 848cc Mini saloon was discontinued. Unlike the Van, more 1-litre Pick-ups than the 850 version were made in the later years.

Specification and performance

As Mini Van, except:

Length	130.2in (3,307mm)
Height	53.5in (1,359mm)
Weight	1,369lb (621kg)
Load capacity	(to waist level) 26.75cu ft (0.76cu m)

Optional extras

Windscreen washer (until 1962)
Seat belts (until 1974)
Interior rear-view mirror
998cc engine with 3.44:1 final drive (from 1967)
Canvas tilt with frame

Range

Austin Se7en Pick-up (1961)
Austin Mini Pick-up (1962–69)
Morris Mini Pick-up (1961–69)
Mini Pick-up 850 (1969–80)
Mini Pick-up 1000 (1969–83)

Production history

As Mini Van, except:
January 1961: Launch of the Pick-up in Austin and Morris versions (Chassis Number AAU7 87551 – Austin, and MAU4 91551 – Morris).
January 1962: Austin version now called Austin Mini Pick-up.
October 1969: All models rebadged as Mini Pick-up.
February 1974: Inertia-reel seat belts standard.
November 1979: 'L' pack not available for Pick-up.
November 1980: Pick-up 850 discontinued.
May 1983: Pick-up 1000 discontinued.
Total production: Austin/Morris Mini Pick-up: 30,652 (of which approx 18,000 Austin and approx 12,500 Morris); Mini Pick-up 850: 12,130; Mini Pick-up 1000: 15,397. Total: 58,179.

Like the Van, the Pick-up retained its old-style Mini features throughout its production life. This 1978 example now had additional strengthening sections between the wheelarch and body top roll. Note that the swing-down number-plate is still there! Production of the 1-litre version ended in 1983.

You would not believe this interior could come from a Mini still made in the Eighties. But both Van and Pick-up retained the 1959-style door bins, sliding windows and single instrument pod to the end. Note the lever-pull door handle and such mod cons as twin stalks, rocker switches and remote gearchange.

Riley Elf and Wolseley Hornet

Two years into the production life of the Mini, most of the major variants on the ADO15 theme had already made their appearance. There was the more luxurious Super Mini, the long-wheelbase estate car and commercials and the Mini-Cooper.

Two much more radical upmarket derivatives arrived in October 1961 in the form of the Riley Elf and the Wolseley Hornet. These were conceived as top-of-the-range small saloons with the 'quality' badges of BMC's most prestigious marques. They undoubtedly provided a small but profitable extra market niche for the all-pervasive Mini formula.

The styling work was done by BMC's 'style guru' of the time, Dick Burzi, who had been responsible for most of the Austins of the Fifties. He was told to bring a dignified air to the Mini. This essentially meant adding all the trappings of the traditional British luxury saloon, which Burzi interpreted as an upright chrome grille, wood veneer dash and a redesigned, lengthened tail.

Although the practical differences between the Riley and Wolseley were minimal, there were the ever-present demands of the BMC sales hierarchy: the Riley Elf was judged to be more upper-crust than the Wolseley Hornet by the most pedantic of margins. To justify its slightly higher price tag, it was fitted with marginally superior trimmings. Each model was sold through entirely different chains of dealers.

The main stylistic differences over the Mini were the addition of the lengthened tail and specific upright grilles. The extended tail made the Elf and Hornet some 8.5in longer than the Mini, although it hardly increased carrying capacity at all; the chief benefit of the new boot was its ability to swallow longer items. The bootlid now hinged conventionally at the top, rather than the base, which negated the Mini's elegantly simple solution of carrying extra luggage (by dropping the tailgate). There was initially some criticism that the boot-stay lacked any counter-balancing and the lid could snap closed without warning. This would be remedied in the MkII of 1963.

Straddling the boot were two miniature fins containing Morris 1100-style pointed rear lights with chrome surrounds. There was also a new wraparound rear bumper which matched the stronger bumper fitted at the front.

The Elf and Hornet both had a unique chrome grille in the traditional style for each marque. The Wolseley acquired its famous illuminated grille badge, while the Riley boasted the traditional 'U' shape along its top edge. A point common to both was the way the grille lifted up with the bonnet. This may have looked good, but it provided the perfect opportunity for a head to make contact

The Riley Elf and Wolseley Hornet (pictured) were a simple attempt to marry the Mini powertrain with the traditional style and luxury of BMC's famous old marques. More than just badge-engineering, these booted Minis were always controversial.

The Riley Elf was a marketing man's dream: essentially a Mini with chrome and fins. The bonnet and nose section were very different from the Mini's, incorporating Riley's traditional U-shaped grille in gleaming chrome. Note that this Elf, pictured at launch in October 1961, has no external seam on its front wing and no bumper overriders. These were features of only the very earliest Elfs.

with it when working in the engine bay. The Elf and Hornet were also the first of the Mini family to gain a lockable bonnet. In addition, both models acquired chrome 'whiskers' in the form of extra cooling grilles beside the main grille.

Another unique difference was the absence – on early models at least – of the Mini's front body seam and the lack of bumper overriders. Both became standard features within six months.

The specifications of the Elf and Hornet were far superior to every other sort of Mini. There was much more chromework on the outside, including the waist strip, window frames, wing trims and wheel embellishers. Each model was available in its unique range of colours (often duo-tone), again capitalizing on the traditional colour schemes of each marque.

Inside, the cabins were much plusher, with standard leather-cloth (and soon leather) seat facings, better seat padding, higher-quality carpets, carpeted door facings, a lidded ashtray and chromed gear-lever. There were detail differences between the Elf and Hornet, the former having slightly more upmarket treatment, notably a full-width wooden dash with lockable boxes either side of the three-gauge instrument binnacle. The Hornet had the standard Cooper-type oval binnacle with a wood veneer finish and no boxed-in dash tray.

These booted Minis must have been anathema to Issigonis. They were the marketing men's dream, painted wagons full of trinkets – and priced up accordingly. The simple idea of a folding bootlid to carry more luggage was utterly nullified by the conventional lid of the Elf and

Hornet (which could only then carry a measly 0.5cu ft more luggage). Opinions were often forthright about the so-called style of the front end. *Car* magazine commented frankly in a test of the Wolseley: "The hideous grille on the front is a mere mockery".

Mechanically, the new twins were identical to the Mini, complete with the 848cc engine, rubber-cone suspension and drum brakes all round. As the Elf and Hornet were considerably heavier than the Mini, this made them rather dull performers, and braking was not a strong suit.

These deficiencies were countered with the introduction of the MkII Elf and Hornet in January 1963. The main change was the fitment

Despite the extra length of the tail, there was not much additional space inside the boot, whose lid hinged at the top. The rear lights, encased in embryonic fins and swathed with chrome, were unique to the Elf and Hornet.

The Elf had a dashboard completely encased in veneer-covered wood (walnut for the twin gloveboxes and central panel). The steering wheel had a Riley badge in its centre. Note the Mini-style door pockets, which stayed with the Elf until it gained winding windows in 1966, and the cranked-over chrome-plated direct-change gear-lever.

of a brand-new 998cc engine, achieved by mating a Morris 1100 block and cylinder head with the crankshaft dimensions of the old 948cc A-series engine. With a single carburettor and the standard 8.3:1 compression ratio, it developed a more healthy 38bhp.

Yet why didn't BMC simply fit the 997cc engine of the Mini-Cooper? Well, this was felt to lack reliability at higher revs (the Cooper would soon also receive the 998cc engine). As the new engine was much 'squarer' than the Cooper unit, it could be revved more freely. In addition, production logistics favoured the already existing Morris 1100 block and the shorter-stroke crank shared with the Morris Minor 1000.

With an extra 4bhp of power and 8lb.ft of torque to tap into, the MkII Elf and Hornet were restored to a performance par with the smaller-engined Mini. The 1-litre engine also had the unplanned benefit of improving fuel economy at higher speeds. Wider front brake drums and twin leading shoes also remedied the weak braking reputation of the booted Minis. Hydrolastic springing was fitted to the Elf and Hornet, as to all Mini saloons, from 1964.

The Elf and Hornet were the first Minis to lose their external door hinges (in October 1966 – some three years before the rest of the range). This coincided with the arrival of the MkIII. At the same time, they also became the first of the British Mini family to gain that other luxury – winding windows. This feature filled in much of the elbow width from door to door, but did not do away with the celebrated door pockets – it just made them much smaller. There were also now conventional-style door handles, a Cooper-type remote gearchange and face-level ventilation.

Automatic transmission, identical to that developed for the Mini, became a popular option for the Elf and the Hornet, although only from 1967.

One final Elf/Hornet variant was a batch of 'beach' cars designed by Dick Burzi. These were doorless cars fitted with wickerwork seats, and intended for export to holiday resorts. A production run never commenced, but as many as 16 beach cars (including Minis) were built by BMC.

Riley and Wolseley became the first victims of the sweeping rationalizations of the post-1968 British Leyland era. As badge-engineered niche models they had to be killed off, and this ceremony was duly performed when the Mini MkIII was launched in 1969.

Despite their historical position as largely unloved members of the large Mini family, many features of the Elf and Hornet – the 998cc engine, wind-up windows, internal door hinges, face-level ventilation – were applied to the standard Mini saloon in years to come, so they could still count on some self-respect, even in their graves.

Riley Elf (1961–69)

The Riley Elf, launched simultaneously with the Wolseley Hornet, was the poshest Mini yet made by BMC. As well as the booted rear end, there was a traditional-style U-shaped Riley chrome grille incorporating a Riley badge, flanked by two side chrome grilles with four horizontal bars each.

The MkII version was externally distinguishable only by its rear chrome 'MkII' badge, but the driving character was significantly improved by the introduction of the new 998cc engine and better braking.

The MkIII came with the distinction of concealed door hinges and wind-up windows. There was a 'MkIII' badge on the tail and some of these late Elfs had hubcaps bearing the Riley trapezoidal badge.

Within a few months of its launch, the Elf had gained fat chrome overriders for the bumpers and the familiar exposed seams of the Mini had made a reappearance. Note the twin air intakes at the front with four horizontal bars – unique to the Riley – the extra chrome trim around the waistline and windows and the contrasting colour roof.

Specification

	MkI	MkII/MkIII
Engine	848cc 4-cyl OHV	998cc 4-cyl OHV
Engine designation	8MB	9WR, 99H
Bore/stroke	62.94 x 68.26mm	64.59 x 76.2mm
Compression ratio	8.3:1	8.3:1
Power output	34bhp at 5,500rpm	38bhp at 5,250rpm
Torque	44lb.ft at 2,900rpm	52lb.ft at 2,700rpm

Transmission
Four-speed manual: Ratios: 4th 3.765, 3rd 5.317, 2nd 8.176, 1st 13.657, Rev 13.657
Four-speed automatic option from 1967: Ratios: 4th 1.0-2.0, 3rd 1.46-2.92, 2nd 1.85-3.7, 1st 2.69-5.38, Rev 2.69-5.38

Steering	Rack & pinion
Brakes	Hydraulic drum/drum
Suspension	Independent

    Front: Wishbones, rubber cones, Armstrong telescopic dampers (Hydrolastic from 1964)
    Rear: Trailing arms, rubber cones, Armstrong telescopic dampers (Hydrolastic from 1964)

Wheels	Pressed steel 3.5 x 10in
Tyres	5.20 x 10in Dunlop C41 cross-ply
Wheelbase	80.2in (2,037mm)
Length	120.25in (3,054mm)
Width	55in (1,397mm)
Height	53in (1,346mm)
Front track	47.4in (1,204mm)
Rear track	45.9in (1,166mm)
Weight	1,393lb (632kg)
Fuel tank	5.5gal (25l)
Luggage capacity	6cu ft (0.17cu m)

Performance

Maximum speed	73mph (118km/h)	77mph (123km/h)
0–50mph	18.3sec	15.7sec
0–60mph	32.3sec	24.1sec
30–50mph	–	11.5sec
40–60mph	–	15.4sec
50–70mph	–	23.1sec
Average fuel consumption	33mpg	35mpg

In 1966, the Elf MkIII made its momentous arrival. It was the first of the Mini family – in Britain, at least – to gain winding windows and concealed door hinges. That meant changing the door handles and the interior door panel, which now contained shrunken door bins.

Optional extras

Whitewall tyres
Weathermaster front tyres
Radio
Fresh-air heater
Steering lock (export only)
Automatic transmission (from 1967)

Plus various approved accessories, such as seat covers, door pocket ashtray, wing mirrors, seat belts, auxiliary lamps, rubber mats.

Range

Riley Elf MkI (1961–62)
Riley Elf MkII (1963–66)
Riley Elf MkIII (1966–69)

Production history

October 1961: Riley Elf introduced (Chassis Number R/A2S1 156851).
April 1962: Front body seams and front and rear bumper overriders fitted as standard.
Autumn 1962: Progressive introduction of baulk-ring synchromesh on upper three gears. Leather replaced leather-cloth on seat facings and rear seats improved.
November 1962: MkI production ceased (final Chassis Number R/A2S1 310706).
January 1963: Elf MkII introduced with new 998cc engine, improved braking, counterbalanced bootlid (Chassis Number R/A2S2 369601). More powerful heater (Body Number FR 3605).
May 1963: Improved catch for sliding windows (Body Number FR 4916).
September 1963: Improved telescopic dampers fitted (Chassis Number R/A2S2 464728).
September 1964: Hydrolastic suspension fitted, plus diaphragm spring clutch, combined starter/ignition switch, crushable sun visors and plastic-framed driving mirror (Chassis Number R/A2S2 639909).
October 1966: Last Elf MkII produced (final Chassis Number R/A2S2 930220). Elf MkIII launched with concealed door hinges, winding windows, revised interior and exterior door handles, reshaped door trims, remote-control gear-lever and fresh-air vents at both ends of facia (Chassis Number R/A2S3 930221).
October 1967: Restyled seats and combined stalk switch on steering column (Chassis Number R/A2S3 1070266). Automatic transmission now offered as an optional extra.
August 1968: Full synchromesh fitted (Engine Number 99H 249 H 101).
August 1969: Last Riley Elf produced (final Chassis Number R/A2S3 1337993).
Total production: Riley Elf MkI: 3,522; Riley Elf Mk II: 17,816; Riley Elf MkIII: 9,574. Total: 30,912.

Wolseley Hornet (1961–69)

The Wolseley Hornet differed only in detail from the Riley Elf, and slotted in at a slightly lower position in the BMC hierarchy. The main distinguishing features were the traditional Wolseley chrome grille with its illuminated badge, side chrome grilles with four vertical bars in addition to the horizontal bars and different badging on the tail.

The interior was rather less well appointed than the Elf's, with exposed parcel shelves – like the Mini – and an oval three-instrument nacelle with a wood veneer finish. A heater and screen washers were standard.

The specification of the Wolseley Hornet was virtually the same as the Elf's. The big difference was the traditional Wolseley chrome grille with its illuminated badge. It had 'cheese grater' chrome grilles to either side.

The MkII version was mechanically much improved, with its 998cc engine and wider brakes with twin leading shoes. The only external distinguishing mark was a new 'MkII' badge on the bootlid.

The MkIII was easily spotted by its concealed door hinges, wind-up windows and new side front air intakes with no vertical bars, which also swivelled open when the face-level vents inside were opened. Some MkIII models had hubcaps embossed with the Wolseley monogram.

Mini-type rear body seams were never featured on the Elf and Hornet and the beefy rear bumper wrapped around the rear wings to the wheel-arches.

Specification and performance
As Riley Elf

Range
Wolseley Hornet MkI (1961–62)
Wolseley Hornet MkII (1963–66)
Wolseley Hornet MkIII (1966–69)

Production history
October 1961: Wolseley Hornet introduced (Chassis Number W/A2S1 156861).
April 1962: Front body seams and front and rear bumper overriders fitted as standard.
Autumn 1962: Progressive introduction of baulk-ring synchromesh on upper three gears. Leather replaced leather-cloth on seat facings and rear seats improved.
November 1962: MkI production ceased (final Chassis Number W/A2S1 320621).
January 1963: Hornet MkII introduced with new

998cc engine, improved braking and counterbalanced bootlid (Chassis Number W/A2S2 367151). More powerful heater fitted.
May 1963: Improved catch for sliding windows (Body Number FW 4989).
September 1963: Improved telescopic dampers fitted (Chassis Number W/A2S2 463935).
September 1964: Hydrolastic suspension fitted, plus diaphragm spring clutch, combined starter/ignition switch, crushable sun visors and plastic-framed driving mirror (Chassis Number W/A2S2 625740).
October 1966: Last Hornet MkII produced (final Chassis Number W/A2S2 927472). Elf MkIII launched with concealed door hinges, winding windows, revised interior door handles, push-button exterior door handles, reshaped door trims, remote-control gear-lever and fresh-air vents at both ends of facia with swivelling front air

intake strakes (Chassis Number W/A2S3 927473).

October 1967: Restyled seats, plastic cooling fan and combined multi-function stalk switch on steering column (Chassis Number W/A2S3 1070204). Automatic transmission now offered as an optional extra.

August 1968: All-synchromesh gearbox fitted (Engine Number 99H 249 H 101).

August 1969: Last Wolseley Hornet produced (final Chassis Number W/A2S3 1337528).

Total production: Wolseley Hornet MkI: 3,166; Wolseley Hornet MkII: 16,785; Wolseley Hornet MkIII: 8,504. Total: 28,455.

This Hornet MkII demonstrates the distinctive characteristics of its Hydrolastic suspension, which was a new fitment from 1964.

The interior of the Wolseley made do with a Cooper-type three-gauge oval instrument pod, albeit covered in burr-walnut for that luxury touch. This MkIII interior included such refinements as face-level ventilation, winding windows and a remote-control gear-lever.

Mini Moke 1964 to date

What BMC created with the Mini Moke was, to put it mildly, uncharacteristic of that conglomerate organization. If the Mini was arresting and advanced, the Mini Moke was off-the-wall and utterly out-of-place.

It all began plausibly enough, with plans laid by Alec Issigonis himself to develop a second car alongside ADO15 (the Mini). It was to use the Mini's mechanical side as its basis to meet the supposed military needs of the British Army. Indeed, the idea seems to have been spawned at the same time as the Mini itself, making what became the Mini Moke the most bizarre of non-identical twins.

The idea must have sounded at least fairly sane to BMC management. A military vehicle contract would have been very lucrative and Issigonis already had some experience in the field, having designed the Nuffield Gutty, which eventually led to the four-wheel-drive Austin Champ – a car which, incidentally, singularly failed to topple the might of the Land-Rover as the Army's choice.

Prototypes of the so-called 'Buckboard' were running in 1959, even before the launch of the Austin Se7en and Morris Mini-Minor. They consisted of punt-type open steel bodies with an 80in wheelbase, which shared only sections of their bulkhead with the Mini itself. Onto these were bolted Alex Moulton's rubber-cone suspension and a bored-out 948cc Mini engine. In 1960, after half a dozen had been hand-built, a Buckboard was shown at a military review and the cars were sent to the Fighting Vehicles Research and Development Establishment at Chertsey – the very place where the Mini had been launched to the press the year before.

The Buckboard was intended to meet the strong military need for a light vehicle which could survive a parachute drop and be lifted by a helicopter. The original prototype weighed a mere 2½cwt and had the added advantage that several could be stacked on top of each other.

Almost immediately it became obvious that the Buckboard was unsuited to the Army's requirements. It was incapable of tackling steep gradients when fully loaded and, crucially, it suffered from a chronic lack of ground clearance, mainly caused by the Moke's tiny wheels, making it useless for off-road work. The Royal Marines and the RAF also gave it the thumbs-down. The only Government agency to show any interest was the Royal Navy, and then only because production of its preferred choice, the UK-built Citroen 2CV pick-up, had ceased.

BMC tried to address the ground clearance problem with a new design on a shortened (72.5in) wheelbase. These prototypes arrived in 1962 and were now referred to as Minimokes ('moke' is a type of packhorse donkey). They had quite different bodywork, with a new front end, but the 948cc engine was retained. BMC's solution to the clearance problem was to add packing to the suspension and put a sump guard under the engine. No-one was very impressed.

The same year, BMC developed an Issigonis-inspired 4x4 Moke by the extraordinary expedient of placing a second engine of 848cc capacity in the tail, a car which came to be referred to as the 'Twini-Moke'. This provided excellent traction and acceleration and was presented as the first-ever eight-cylinder Austin (with a total capacity of 1,696cc!), but potential customers thought a four-wheel-drive car with poor ground clearance no more interesting than a two-wheel-drive one. Even the American army tested a Twini-Moke (with two 1,100cc engines), to no consequence.

Having found no interest whatsoever for the Moke as a military machine, BMC decided to cut its losses, return to the 80in wheelbase format and develop a version for civilian use during 1963.

After the first Buckboard prototypes, BMC built this short-wheelbase Mini Moke for military applications, but not one military body placed an order.

This Mini Moke prototype, built by Issigonis in 1962, had two A-series engines, one at the front and one at the back, creating a novel four-wheel-drive vehicle. The car was dubbed the Twini-Moke.

Basic in the extreme, this was the original Mini Moke in production form. Even passenger seats were optional extras, since the Moke was classed as a commercial vehicle.

Due to production logistics, it was decided to use the standard 848cc Mini engine with as many mechanical parts as possible taken from the Mini, including its subframes, suspension, steering and brakes.

Production began in January 1964 and the initial reaction of the motoring world was one of puzzlement. What was this machine? Who was it intended for? Why was it on sale at all? Journals struggled to find suggested uses for it: as hotel courtesy transport, as a beach car, golf cart, factory transport.... Road tests by the likes of *Autocar* or *Motor* were thin on the ground, and the Moke received more interest from publications like BMC's own *Payload* magazine, reflecting the Moke's intended role as a workhorse.

Construction was a simple unitary rustproofed steel body built up on rudimentary jigs at Longbridge. The Mini Moke was fitted with a windscreen which could fold flat or be removed completely, there was a stout bumper bar at each

end and the simple bonnet could be unclasped from its rubber clips and removed completely. The spare wheel was bolted in true military style on the rump.

A vinyl-treated fabric tilt roof supported by removable poles was standard, but weather protection in the form of side screens came as an extra. The Moke was sold initially with only one seat, which had a removable padded cover to expose the metal seat frame for heavy-duty work. If it was intended to carry passengers, seats had to be bought as extras, including grab handles. Interestingly, the law at that time stated that without passenger seats, a speed of 40mph could not be exceeded, so people in a hurry had to go for the seat option!

Storage space was not a problem – it could be argued that the whole car was one big storage space. Security was not, however, a Moke strong suit. On one side, panels on the chunky sill boxes could be removed to reveal cubbyholes in which were also stored the battery and tools; on the opposite side was the petrol tank.

The instrument panel with its single dial was basic in the extreme. There was only one windscreen wiper – a second wiper requiring an extra motor was an option – and the Moke could be purchased in any colour desired – so long as it was Spruce Green.

As introduced, the Moke was sold as a commercial vehicle alongside the Van and Pick-up. Even in 1994, the Moke was not homologated in Britain as a four-seater passenger car and so was being sold with only two seats, the rear ones remaining an optional extra. The 1964 Moke

The Moke's target market was the rural community, but trendy Londoners bought most of them. Note the grab handles fitted for the rear passengers and the single windscreen wiper.

attracted purchase tax at the commercial rate and it slotted in as the cheapest four-wheeled car on the British market at a mere £405.

Yet in truth, the Mini Moke was not a car for the British market. Some were bought by building site operators, some by fire brigades, and even the AA test-ran a Moke. Fewer than 10 per cent of production was sold in the UK, most being destined for sunnier climes, almost exclusively as tourist courtesy and hire cars. The well-known conversion specialists Crayford developed a Surrey Moke with a stripey roof and trim, which became the normal treatment for the Moke in such sub-tropical destinations.

The Moke was too basic, too crude, too slow and too cold for British buyers. As *Motoring Which* put it, "Driving through the back streets of Kensington in pouring rain in the Moke must rate, as an activity, very low on anyone's fun index". However, it did attract some attention from the Carnaby Street 'in-crowd' and became something of a cult object – especially after Patrick McGoohan's TV series, *The Prisoner*, in which brightly-adorned Surrey Mokes appeared.

In the event, the British tax authorities effectively put paid to the Mini Moke in 1967 by reclassing it as a passenger car for tax purposes. This raised the cost of a Moke by £78 and suddenly it did not look so good alongside cheaper, more civilized cars. The novelty had rather worn off, too, and so BMC abandoned British production in 1968, with some 14,518 built, of which only 1,467 had been sold on the home market. All Mini Mokes, both Austin and

Morris, had been built at the Longbridge works.

At that stage, limited production of the Mini Moke had already begun in Australia – since 1966, in fact – at BMC's Sydney plant. However, from 1968, Australia became the sole manufacturing location for Mokes. Early examples retained the 10in wheels and were initially fitted with bigger 998cc engines to suit Aussie conditions better.

Australia was really a much better place to build Mokes. The climate was willing and soon BMC Australia was making its own modifications to suit its market. A Mk2 version was introduced with the 1,098cc A-series engine from the domestic Mini K saloon fitted as standard, but more important was the change to 13in wheels, which looked a natural fitment on the Moke. This raised ground clearance by a small but significant amount. It also meant fitting wider tyres, in turn leading to the expansion of the wheelarches by an inch or so all round. Unfortunately, the cost of getting extra ground clearance was the necessity of developing parts specifically for the Moke: special rear trailing arms had to be fitted, as did a different steering rack and a unique final drive.

Other changes included a slightly loftier height, standard tow-bar, an improved cooling system, rubber CV joint protectors and an integral sump guard. Parcel shelves were added either side of the speedo panel, and it came with a steering lock – security had never been a Moke strong suit – plastic mudflaps and Perspex front quarter-lights. A pick-up – or 'tray top' in Antipodean parlance – was also offered from 1974.

Unlike the British Moke, the Antipodean version managed to score sales with the Armed Forces: the Australian Army bought over 500 in 1972 and other customers included many overseas bases and the New Zealand Navy (which to this day carries Mokes on its ships).

In the civilian market, it sold respectably because it slotted in as Australia's cheapest car, being sold with the line: "Moking is Not a Wealth Hazard". The Moke in Australia was treated for many years as much more of a farmers' 'rough and tumble' machine for bush work, but gradually became softer as it was realized that it could not compete with the small Daihatsu and Suzuki off-roaders which assaulted the Australian market in the Seventies.

Launched initially as a special edition, the Moke Californian eventually became a production model, available alongside the basic Moke. It typified the move towards a softer approach. The first Californian of 1971 was sold only with the 1,275cc engine. Later versions had big nerf bars front and rear, full weather gear, a standard rollbar, white spoked wheels and better seats.

Some of these Mokes even made it back to Britain, where a firm called Runamoke imported several hundred through the Seventies and early Eighties. In export terms, the Australian Moke was a great success: it was sold in 82 countries and some 35 per cent of production was exported.

Leyland Australia could even afford a little humour for the cheapest car on the market. In the Seventies, it was available in a range of bright colours with names like Scarlet O'Hara, Yellow Devil and Hairy Lime. One later edition of the Californian came with a blue denim-look hood and seats.

Yet the Australian Moke was doomed. On grounds of cost, Leyland Australia reverted to using the less powerful 998cc engine – in emissions-restricted form – as the standard fitment, then ceased to offer the 1,275cc unit even as an option (although it did come back once again). One magazine suggested that the car's crudity, inadequacy off-road, sluggardliness and high price should earn it the name 'Joke', not Moke.

Australian production ceased in 1981, with some 26,142 cars built. A four-wheel-drive Moke and a sportscar-bodied Moke – called the Gran Turismoke! – were scuppered and the old plant was given over to the manufacture of Peugeots.

It appears that production of Mokes had already begun in Portugal by this stage. CKD kits from

With its hood erected, the Moke was weatherproof – just.

Australia were being built up into complete cars at the British Leyland-owned Industria Montagem factory in Setubal as early as 1980. This appears to have amounted to an attempt by British Leyland Portugal to get around import restrictions: if a manufacturer produced cars locally, it could import more cars. A clever way of selling Metros in Portugal was to produce the Moke – a car which could be put together without setting up a conventional production line and using relatively unskilled labour.

No frills whatever adorned the Moke's interior. A basic metal panel containing the familiar Mini speedometer, plus switches for the lights and a choke control.

133

This 1965 Morris-badged prototype for a pick-up body based on the Moke looked promising. A Pick-up Moke would enter production in Australia in the Seventies.

One of the most famous settings for the Mini Moke: a shot from the 1967 cult TV series, *The Prisoner*, with Patrick McGoohan at the wheel.

Production in earnest did not begin until 1983, when the Moke Californian was produced, but fitted with a 40bhp 998cc engine (the mechanical side of the Moke was always imported from Britain). The specification included Aussie-style 13in white spoked wheels, a full rollcage, nerf bars, high-back seats with headrests, full weather gear and so on.

Austin Rover in Britain thought the Moke stood a good chance of finding customers in the UK and tendered a concessionary contract. Kit car makers Dutton Cars won and began selling new Moke Californians in Britain in late 1983 from £4,100. However, only around a dozen were sold by Dutton, as production and customs problems overcame the import attempt.

The Portuguese factory suffered from poor industrial relations and was declared bankrupt in late 1984. Production restarted under a new regime headed by Jim Lambert, a retired BL executive who had had experience with the Australian Moke. The new company was still majority-owned by Austin Rover. A new manu-facturing site was found in an ex-MAN truck factory in Vendas Novas (100 miles from Lisbon) and a series of specification changes began to be instituted. The idea was to rationalize production around as many standard Mini parts as possible. Hence, Mini 12in wheels were standardized, the low-compression 998cc engine was retained alongside an economy gearbox, standard 3.44:1 differential and disc brakes. From 1986, the rear mudguards were returned to their original width.

Austin Rover's involvement looked set to relax as Portugal joined the EC and import quotas were abolished, allowing the firm to sell its products freely without having recourse to its factory in Portugal – the original reason why Austin Rover had been so keen to make the Moke in Portugal.

Yet production was suddenly looking very healthy: from an annual average of about 2,000 Mokes a year, sales leapt to over 3,500 in 1987, with particularly strong sales in France, Spain, Japan and Italy. Yet following the collapse of some hefty fleet orders, Rover tired of the Moke and finally called a halt to production in 1989, putting the project up for sale, despite the fact that the operation was profitable and had outstanding orders. Some 1,230 cars had been built in the final year of Austin Rover production.

The strong sales of Mokes in Italy eventually proved fateful. Ownership of the Moke project transferred in 1990 to the Italian motorbike maker Cagiva, of Bologna, which set up a subsidiary called Moke Automobili SpA. Rover actually sold the Moke name to Cagiva – a rare instance of a manufacturer selling a trade name – and the model would henceforth be called just 'Moke'.

Production recommenced in 1991, with virtually no specification changes, at the Portugal works at a production rate of approximately half that of the previous regime: 1,226 cars in 1991, followed by 725 in 1992. However, Cagiva decided that its interests would be better served if it took up spare capacity in its own motorcycle factories in Italy and so called a halt to Portuguese production at the end of 1993, transferring all tooling to Italy where, at the time of writing, a production line is still being set up. Manufacture is set to recommence in early 1995, using catalyzed 1,275cc Rover engines.

In Britain, the Moke was imported by the Duncan Hamilton group from 1988. They had somewhat better luck with the Moke than Dutton, having sold around 400 cars in the UK by 1994. Total Moke production to the end of 1992 came to 9,277 cars.

Austin and Morris Mini Moke (1964–68)

The Mini Moke was launched after a five-year gestation period in 1964 as a civilian workhorse. Its specification was basic in the extreme, mirroring its intended market as a commercial vehicle.

Mechanically, the Mini Moke was almost identical to the Mini saloon: it used the complete subframe assemblies from the standard 848cc Mini – albeit tuned to run on low-grade fuel – but its gearbox had different ratios, notably with the higher 3.44:1 final drive of the Mini-Cooper.

With the ever-important marque distinctions prevailing at BMC, there were Austin and Morris versions of the Mini Moke, although the sole difference between the marques was the badge above the front grille.

The Mini Moke was always something of a specialist product and hence received little in the way of development. It was never provided with Hydrolastic suspension, despite having a virtually identical wheelbase to the saloons: it was always viewed as a load carrier by BMC, and so was unsuited to a fluid suspension system.

The Mini Moke as produced in Britain was essentially an export special: 90 per cent of all production went abroad and a mere 1,467 examples were sold in Britain.

Specification

Engine	848cc four-cylinder OHV
Bore/stroke	62.94 x 68.26mm
Compression ratio	8.3:1
Power output	34bhp at 5,500rpm
Torque	44lb.ft at 2,900rpm
Transmission	Four-speed manual: Ratios: 4th 3.44, 3rd 4.86, 2nd 7.47, 1st 12.48
Steering	Rack & pinion
Brakes	Drum/drum
Suspension	Independent with dry rubber cones
Wheels	3.5 x 10in pressed steel
Tyres	5.20 x 10in Dunlop C41 cross-ply
Wheelbase	79.9in (2,029mm)
Length	120in (3,048mm)
Width	51.5in (1,308mm)
Height	56in (1,422mm)
Front track	47.45in (1,205mm)
Rear track	45.85in (1,165mm)
Weight	1,176lb (534kg)
Fuel tank	6.25gal (28l)

Performance

Maximum speed	65mph (105km/h)
0–50mph	15.4sec
0–60mph	21.8sec
Average fuel consumption	33mpg

Optional extras

Passenger seats and grab handles
Side screens
Extra windscreen wiper and motor
Windscreen washer
Laminated windscreen
Sump guard
Dunlop Weathermaster tyres
Heater

Range

Austin Mini Moke (1964–68)
Morris Mini Moke (1964–68)

Production history

January 1964: Production of Austin Mini Moke began (Chassis Number A/AB1 513101). One Morris Mini Moke produced in first batch with Chassis Number M/AB1 513106.
June 1964: Production of Morris Mini Moke began (Chassis Number M/AB1 604305).
August 1964: Austin and Morris Mini Moke available in Britain. Cost: £405.
October 1968: Production of both versions of the Mini Moke ceased at Longbridge.
Total production: Austin Mini Moke: 5,422; Morris Mini Moke: 9,096. Total: 14,518.

Australia:
BMC Morris Mini Moke (1966–68), BMC Mini Moke (1968–70), BMC Moke (1970–72) and Leyland Moke (1972–81)

The Australian-produced Moke began life in 1966 as essentially a British Mini Moke assembled under licence with a 998cc engine. Gradually it developed into a machine more suited to Antipodean needs and, from 1968, Australia became the sole manufacturing source of Mokes.

In 1968 13in wheels became available as an option, but were soon standardized on the Mk2 version because Australian drivers appreciated the extra ground clearance.

The original Californian of 1971 was aimed at younger buyers, with a variety of colour schemes, better seats and a multi-coloured Paisley-pattern vinyl soft-top. It was the first Moke to be available with the 1,275cc engine, which was the only available engine for the first-series Moke and was supplied from Longbridge in Britain. This was the only Moke to be fitted with a rear-mounted fuel tank and filler.

The Californian name was revived in 1977 in a high-spec version of the standard Moke. It had such features as wide white-spoked wheels, bull bars, rubber floor mats, alloy-spoke steering wheel and 'Californian' decals on the bonnet. In some editions, one could even be acquired with a denim-style hood and seats.

Performance
Maximum speed   70mph (113km/h)
Average fuel consumption   33mpg

Optional extras
Roll-over cage (standard Moke only from 1979)
Headlamp mesh guards
Side screens
Wintertread tyres (standard Moke only)
1,275cc engine (Californian only)
Metallic paint (Californian only)
Heater/demister
Radio
6.00 x 13in tyres
5.60 x 13in Weathermaster tyres

Range
BMC Morris Mini Moke (1966–68)
BMC Mini Moke (1968–70)
BMC Moke (1970–72)
BMC Moke Californian (1971–73)
Leyland Moke (1972–81)
Leyland Moke Utility (1974–81)
Leyland Moke Californian (1977–81)

In Australia, the Moke received 13in wheels and a bigger engine. In order for the rear wings to clear the larger wheels, the rear panel had to be kicked out.

Specification

	998	1098	1,275
Engine	998cc 4-cyl	1,098cc 4-cyl	1,275cc 4-cyl
Bore/stroke	64.59 x 76.2mm	64.59 x 83.7mm	70.61 x81.28
Compression ratio	8.3:1	8.5:1	8.8:1
Power output	38bhp at 5,250rpm 40bhp (from 1976)	50bhp at 5,100rpm	65bhp at 5,250rpm 54bhp (from 1979)
Torque	52lb.ft at 2,700rpm	60lb.ft at 2,500rpm	69lb.ft at 2,500rpm 67lb.ft from 1979
Transmission	Four-speed manual: Ratios 4th 4.1, 3rd 5.8, 2nd 8.8, 1st 15.0; or: 4th 4.267, 3rd 6.13, 2nd 9.471, 1st 15.056, Rev 15.129		
Steering	Rack & pinion		
Brakes	Drum/drum Disc/drum on Californian (from 1979)		
Suspension	Independent by rubber cones		
Wheels	10 x 3.5in, 13 x 4.5in (from 1968)		
Tyres	5.20-10in cross-ply; 5.60-13in (from 1968) 6.15-13in (1971–73 Californian) Wintertread 175 R13 radial-ply (1977–81 Californian)		
Wheelbase	82.5in (2,096mm)		
Length	127.25in (3,232mm) Pick-up: 144.2in (3,663mm)		
Width	57in (1,488mm) Pick-up: 59.5in (1,511mm)		
Height	63in (1,600mm) Pick-up: 68.5in (1,739mm)		
Front track	47.75in (1,213mm) – 1966–68 48.1in (1,222mm) – 1968–69 49in (1,245mm) – from 1969		
Rear track	46.9in (1,190mm) – 1966–68 49.2in (1,250mm) – 1968–69 49.75in (1,264mm) – from 1969		
Weight	Moke (1966): 1,255lb (570kg) Moke: 1,367lb (621kg) Californian: 1,509lb (686kg) Pick-up: 1,588lb (722kg)		
Fuel tank	6.25gal (28.4l) – 8.4gal (38l) from 1979 Californian (1971–73): 6gal (27l)		

Production history

February 1966: Morris Mini Moke first launched in Australia with 998cc engine. Cost: $1,295.
1968: 13in wheels first offered. Name changed to BMC Mini Moke.
April 1969: Mk2 Moke arrived: standard engine became the 1,098cc A-series and 13in wheels were standard. Also wider tracks, larger mudguards, kicked-out rear panel, better oil filter, improved cooling, larger brake cylinders, lower final drive and Cooper 'S' type mechanical inboard universal joints.
1970: Name changed to BMC Moke.
December 1971: Moke Californian launched with 1,275cc engine, two-speed wipers, hazard flashers, reversing light, spare wheel cover and rear-mounted fuel tank. Cost: $1,675.

April 1972: Name changed to Leyland Moke.
1973: 1,275cc engine dropped because of emissions regulations, taking the Californian with it.
December 1974: Moke Utility (pick-up) launched. Cost: $2,377. Production ceased at Sydney plant.
April 1975: Production restarted at Enfield plant.
May 1975: 1,098cc engine deleted. Mokes now only with 998cc engine.
1976: Emissions-controlled 998cc engine introduced.
September 1977: Uprated Moke Californian launched with 998cc engine and uprated equipment. Cost: $3,599.
November 1979: Moke revamped with zinc galvanized body, improved front deflector screens, new hood with zippered side screens,

new high-back tilting front seats, strengthened spare wheel bracket, larger fuel tank with side-mounted filler, new rollover cage for Californian, inertia-reel seat belts, new stalk-mounted controls (similar to Triumph TR7), improved gearchange, improved mountings for bumpers, modified steering rack, improved emissions control, larger front grille badge and new 'Moke' logo on rear mudflaps. Mokes also available with detoxed 1,275cc engine.

November 1981: Moke production ceased in Australia.

Total production: 26,142.

The Australian-assembled 1971 Californian Moke, demonstrating how the model softened during the Seventies: patterned seats and hood and, later, decals and white spoked wheels.

Throughout the Seventies, the Moke was Australia's cheapest car. From 1974, a 'tray top' (Pick-up) version was also offered.

Portugal: Mini Moke (1980–89) and Moke (1991–94)

The Portuguese-made Moke began life as the Australian-specification Moke Californian, merely supplanted to a new manufacturing location. It used the 998cc 39bhp A-plus engine supplied in what was dubbed a 'Powerpack' from Longbridge in Britain: Mini subframe assemblies complete with brakes, steering, suspension, some instruments and so on.

From 1984, the Moke began to change its specification towards the more cost-effective solution of using more standard British Mini parts. Hence, the Mini Moke quickly received 12in wheels and disc front brakes in line with the Mini and a standard final drive.

Improvements followed in the design of the rollover cage and weather protection. Bull bars were standard front and rear and the body panels eventually became fully-galvanized. The interior was much improved with attractive seats and there was a lockable rear boot of sorts.

When production restarted under new owners Cagiva, the 'Mini' was taken out of Moke as Rover was no longer involved and all markings were changed accordingly, including new embossed 'Moke' logos in the seats.

In the UK, an upmarket Moke was also sold alongside the standard model: this was the Moke SE, basically a normal Moke with all the options added: alloy wheels, tinted glass, special nudge bars, metallic paint and so on. Air conditioning was even offered as an option! At the time of writing, production is suspended pending the relocation of the tooling to Italy.

The first Mokes built in Portugal were Australian-specification Californians built from CKD kits. These had alloy wheels and special white nudge bars. From 1983, Dutton Cars imported Mokes into the UK, but without much success.

Specification

Engine	998cc four-cylinder OHV
Bore/stroke	64.58 x 76.2mm
Compression ratio	8.3:1
Power output	39bhp at 4,750rpm
Torque	50lb.ft at 2,500rpm
Transmission	Four-speed manual: Ratios: (From 1984): 4th 3.44, 3rd 4.93, 2nd 7.63, 1st 12.13 From 1989: 4th 3.105, 3rd 4.42, 2nd 6.78, 1st 11.32, Rev 11.38
Steering	Rack & pinion
Brakes	Drum/drum (Disc/drum from 1984)
Suspension	Independent front, double wishbones with rubber cones and telescopic dampers Independent rear, trailing arms with rubber cones and telescopic dampers
Wheels	12 x 4.5in (from 1984)
Tyres	145/70 SR-12 (from 1984)
Wheelbase	80.1in (2,035mm)

From 1985, Austin Rover instituted some production rationalization for the Moke in Portugal including the use of Longbridge-built Mini 'power packs', 12in wheels, front disc brakes and a new roll-over frame.

The Mini Moke 25 was an anniversary edition launched in 1989 and consisting of nothing more elaborate than a set of decals for the bonnet.

This is the penultimate Moke produced by Austin Rover Portugal in 1989.

Under new owners, Cagiva of Italy, production restarted in 1991. The Moke's UK importer sold this high-specification SE model alongside a more basic version.

Length	127.2in (3,232mm)
Width	56.7in (1,440mm)
Height	57.5in (1,460mm)
Front track	49.8in (1,265mm)
Rear track	47.8in (1,215mm)
Weight	1,385lb (630kg)
Fuel tank	8.6gal (39l)
Luggage capacity	–

Performance

Maximum speed	81mph (130km/h)
0–50mph	–
0–60mph	27.9sec
30–50mph	–
40–60mph	–
50–70mph	–
Average fuel consumption	38mpg
Government fuel test (Urban/56mph/75mph)	40.3/37.6/–

Optional extras
Heater
Air conditioning
Alloy wheels
Tinted glass
Sump guard
Towing equipment
Stereo
Spare wheel cover
Hood bag
Custom trim and interior, including leather
Special paintwork
Rear seats
Rear seat belts
Lead-free engine conversion
Hardtop (factory-approved) – from 1993

Range
Mini Moke Californian (1980–85)
Mini Moke (1985–89)
Mini Moke 25 (1989)
Moke (1991 to date)
Moke SE (1991 to date)

Production history
1980: Assembly of Mini Moke Californian began in Portugal using CKD kits sourced from Australia.
Late 1983: UK imports began through Dutton Cars. Cost: £4,100.
December 1984: Production ceased as British Leyland Portugal went into liquidation.
January 1985: Production transferred to new site (Chassis Number TW7XKFP 318 S 580001). No longer called Californian, but retained 13in wheel format throughout 1985. Modified during 1985 to include 12in wheels, flush back panel, disc front brakes and 3.44:1 final drive.
1986: Rear mudguards narrowed by 1in each side.
Late 1986: New hood and seats. Rollbar, grab handles, bumpers and grille now painted silver.
January 1988: Zinc plated body standard. Bumpers now painted white and rollcage painted in body colour. Inertia-reel rear seat belts mounted to rollcage.

Late 1988: UK imports restarted under Duncan Hamilton.

Late 1988: Split rear seats introduced.

May 1989: Moke 25 limited edition (250 stated) launched, with 'Moke 25' decals on bonnet.

July 1989: Rover suspended Portuguese production (final Chassis Number TW7XKFP 328 S 981230).

April 1990: Rights to Moke sold to Italian firm Cagiva.

April 1991: Production restarted under the 'Moke' name, with revised side curtains, radiator resited at the front, electric fan and white trim with green piping (Chassis Number TX5XKFP 318 S 190001).

May 1991: Moke relaunched in UK through Duncan Hamilton in standard and SE forms. Cost: £6,128 and £6,869 respectively.

Late 1993: Production suspended and tooling transferred to Italy.

Total production: From1983 to end of 1992: 9,277.

The interior of the Cagiva-built Moke was fractionally better-equipped than the 1964 version: three instruments, four rocker switches, twin stalk controls and two oddments trays.

One of the last Mokes built in Portugal, with its revised hood whose 'doors' unfolded fore to aft, rather than vertically as before.

International Minis

The Mini is essentially a British institution, but it is safe to say that its continuing popularity abroad has kept it alive until today. When it looked as though the Mini might be axed in the mid-Eighties, it was strong demand from France, Germany and Japan which persuaded Austin Rover to keep it going.

Minis have been exported without a break since 1959, and they have also been made abroad from the earliest days. Right from the start, BMC sent out complete knocked-down (CKD) kits to its assembly operations in dozens of Commonwealth countries around the world.

On the other hand, sometimes whole assembly lines were set up abroad to make Minis. Often, the design of the Mini was adapted to suit local conditions, an early example being the Australian production facility, which introduced Minis with winding windows years before the Longbridge plant adopted them.

The other most famous manufacturing operation was in Italy, where Innocenti, the makers of the Lambretta scooter, built Minis from 1965. This included the estate and the Mini-Cooper.

Production lines were also set up in Spain (under the AUTHI banner), in Belgium (at BL's Seneffe plant) and in South Africa, where a number of variants were built, including the unique 'booted' Mini MkII, essentially a Riley Elf rear end with a normal Mini nose. Production in Chile and Venezuela concentrated on another unique Mini with modified glassfibre bodywork.

The Mini has been alternatively badged in foreign markets: for example, the Mini in Denmark was known as the Morris Mascot because the name Mini was already registered by another firm in that market. The estate was known as the Kombi in Germany, and as the Combi in Switzerland. Initially, the Mayfair was badged in Germany as the Mayfair Sport. Special editions have also been known by different names: the Advantage was sold as the Mini Masters in Germany, for example.

Minis have consistently been adapted to the requirements of foreign markets. For instance, Canadian-specification Minis had extra-powerful heaters, emissions control equipment and, by the late Seventies, extraordinary high-mounted bumpers. The American market, exploited until 1967, could have Minis with big 'cow bars' at the front.

There have also been many special editions unique to foreign markets: for example, the Printemps and After Eight in France, and the Ebony in the Netherlands.

Yet of all Mini export markets, it is Japan that has proven to be the most enthusiastic and has become the biggest export market for the Mini: in 1993, a total of 8,508 cars were sold. That means that it was not only the best-selling British car in Japan by a mile, but that more Minis were sold in Japan than the UK (where 6,326 were sold in

This Japanese-specification Morris Mini 1000 is typical of the modifications made to export Minis to suit local demands. Japanese law in the Seventies required the fitment of twin wing mirrors and extra indicators mounted to the front wings and under the front bumper.

The Mini as sold in Canada in 1975 was bizarre. The Heath Robinson-like arrangement of the bumpers satisfied North American safety laws and extra indicators had to be fitted to the front and rear wings.

1993). The Mini slots in as the cheapest imported car on the Japanese market (in March 1994 it was retailing at £9,200). There is more than just a cult following for the Mini in Japan: it is nothing short of a mania. Young people are swayed by the Mini's authentic and pure appearance, its legendary road behaviour and its low price.

One of the most celebrated of the Japanese fads is the retro-look Mini. Brand-new Minis from Longbridge are decked out with dealer-fitted reproduction items to make your Nineties Mini look like an authentic car from the Sixties. Obviously, the Mini-Cooper 'S' is the car to copy and there are parts available to transform the Mini into an almost exact replica: original-style grilles, 10in ventilated steel wheels, wing-mounted chrome mirrors, even the old centrally-mounted oval instrument nacelle.

The best market for the Mini after Japan is Germany – with an average annual sale around 4,000 – with strong sales also still being recorded in France and Italy.

Export Minis

Right from the beginning in 1959, the Mini has been sent abroad, nearly always with different specifications from the UK-market Mini.

Obviously, export Minis were available with left-hand drive and speedometers calibrated in kilometres, but there were numerous special fittings for foreign markets: a six-blade fan and different lighting, for example.

BMC initially listed two models for export sales: the De Luxe and the Super De Luxe, which were often sold as the Austin or Morris 850 and Super 850, without referring to the name Mini. The early export Super De Luxe was basically the same as the UK-spec De Luxe except that there was a choice of carpets or rubber mats and a heater was optional. The export De Luxe had a non-adjustable passenger seat, woven cloth seats, rubber mats, no ashtray or interior light and no rubber boot mat.

The Mini even made it to the USA. This Morris was pressed into service by the law enforcement authorities in Nevada.

With the arrival of the Super models in 1961, the export range was revised to encompass four models: basic, Export Saloon, De Luxe and Super De Luxe. These variants roughly corresponded to the trim levels offered in Britain. The exception was the Export Saloon, which was an interim model with the same specification as the basic model, but with twin sun visors, hinged rear quarter-lights, chrome exterior trim and a windscreen washer. There was a choice of fresh air or recirculatory heaters as options for all models. Another unique option was the availability of Weathermaster tyres (for the front wheels only).

For 1963, the De Luxe was deleted and the Export Saloon's specification was slightly upgraded to become the sole 'in-between' model with, for example, tubular bumper extensions.

With the introduction of the Mini MkII in 1967, there remained three trim levels: basic, Export Saloon and SDL. The latter had the 998cc engine, corresponding with the UK-market 1000 Super De Luxe. Above the basic model – equivalent to the UK base Mini – the Export was a special model with extra items like wheeltrims, chrome bumpers, plastic screen finishers, hinged rear windows, carpets, twin visors, adjustable passenger's seat and a rear ashtray. Heaters were still extras on all models, as were a radio, laminated windscreen, reclining front seats, a heated rear window, an alternator and the option of automatic transmission.

As the range changed its name to Mini in 1969, export markets acquired additional models: there was an 850 Special De Luxe as well as the basic model and a cheaper 1000 De Luxe in addition to the 1000 Super De Luxe. There were now options of a steering lock, and face-level ventilation, and a heater was still an option on all models. The 850 SDL and 1000 DL had been deleted by 1974.

Export markets also received the Mini Clubman and 1275 GT, also with unique export options like a steering column lock and laminated windscreen.

From 1977 to 1979, there was also a 1300 Special made only for export countries. This was a saloon bodyshell fitted with a 1,275cc engine, and was never seen in Britain. The total number made was 31,360. Continental Minis have consistently been badged with the name 'Special'. The model known as the City was almost always known in export markets as the Mini Special; today's Sprite is still called the Special in Europe.

The differences between home-market and export Minis gradually closed so that the only distinguishing features became the position of the steering wheel, speedo calibration and whatever details local laws required.

Manufacture abroad: Belgian Minis

Belgium quickly became one of the largest manufacturers of Minis outside Britain. At BL's plant in Seneffe, a large variety of Minis was built, one of the most important being the Innocenti Mini-Cooper 1300 Export, made in Belgium from 1973.

There were several Minis unique to Belgian manufacture. The Mini Special was one of the most popular Mini variants on the Continent, being basically a standard bodyshell fitted with the 1,098cc Clubman engine and different trim and badging. The 1100 Special was built at Seneffe from 1977 to 1981 in a run which totalled some 73,753 cars. A further run of 5,100 1100 Specials was made in Britain in 1979 (the limited edition 1100S).

Australian Minis

Australia was one of the Mini's early export markets, but very soon, BMC's operation down under began assembling and part-manufacturing Minis (from March 1961). These were essentially the same as Longbridge Minis, with 848cc engines and standard specifications, and were known as

In Belgium, thousands of the so-called Mini Special were built between 1977 and 1981 for sale in continental Europe. It had a 1,098cc engine, special wheels, vinyl or painted contrasting roof, different badging, 1275 GT-style instruments and extra indicators on the front wings.

Minis made at the Austin Morris plant at Seneffe, in Belgium, await final collection as the plant closes down in April 1981.

Morris 850s (the name Mini Minor was not officially used by BMC Australia until June 1965).

Gradually, more content was made in Australia, and unique features crept in. The most celebrated of these were the wind-up windows introduced in 1965. Unlike later British Minis, which used the Elf/Hornet type of winding window, Australian Minis had hinging front quarter-lights in chrome surrounds and a smaller winding front window. The Deluxe model – launched in March 1965 – had Hydrolastic suspension, key starting and better seats. Australian production of the Minivan also began from May 1965 with the unique feature of wind-up windows.

Automatic transmission was made available on the Australian market in January 1968 (where it was known as the Mini-Matic). The 998cc engine became available from October 1967, mirroring Longbridge, although the MkII model was not launched until September 1968, and then still with the old-style grille.

Locally-built Mini-Coopers were available down

In 1969, BLMC Australia launched a Mini with 80 per cent local content and a 1,098cc engine, which it called the Mini K. Kangaroo badges drove the point home.

Australian Minis were characterized by their early fitment of winding windows of a quite different conception from the later British items. External door hinges were retained until the end of Australian production in 1978. This is a Mini S from the late Seventies.

under from October 1962. The 1,275cc Cooper 'S' was launched in September 1965 with a broadly similar specification to the UK-built 'S'. This was a rather costly car in Australia at $2,280 (almost twice the price of the standard Mini).

From late 1969 there was a new model, the Morris Mini K. The 'K' was a reference to the Kangaroo motifs used on the model, denoting that this was a car with 80 per cent Australian-made content. The standard engine was the 1,098cc A-series unit developing 51bhp and there was superior trim and different instruments. Hydrolastic suspension was fitted to all models at this time, when BMC claimed the Mini was taking 30 per cent of the Australian small car market. The Cooper 'S' MkII was launched in May 1969, with bolt-on flared wheelarches.

The Clubman-style nose arrived in Australia in August 1971, supplanting all other Minis, and so the model was renamed the Mini Clubman 1100, while the Cooper 'S' was replaced by the Mini Clubman GT (with a 1,275cc engine). Unlike British cars, the Clubman retained the old external door hinges until the end and were fitted with Hydrolastic until April 1973.

In April 1972, the Morris name was dropped in favour of the Leyland tag and the model names were changed the following year to just Mini and Mini S. To cut costs and to comply with local emissions laws, Leyland decided in 1975 to switch back from the locally-made 1,098cc engine to the 998cc unit, which it imported from Britain.

In October 1976, a limited run of 500 Mini SS models was launched: these had alloy wheels, twin-speaker stereo, superior trim and SS badging for a 10 per cent premium. This was followed in 1977 by the Mini Sunshine, another limited edition with a full-length folding sunroof, special badging and tinted windows.

The final, and most desirable, Aussie Minis were the LS models. The first version, which joined the Mini S as a regular production model, was the 998cc Mini LS of March 1977. Based on the S, it added a number of items, notably magnesium wheels, a radio/cassette player and metallic paint. This was followed by the Mini 1275 LS in August 1978, which distinguished itself with usefully improved performance and 12in wheels (the first and last Aussie Mini to be so treated).

Unfortunately, the 1275 LS was to be a very rare model as Leyland Australia, faced with spectacular losses caused by the fiasco of its big P76 saloon and rapidly declining Mini sales, gave up making Minis at its Enfield, NSW plant in October 1978. A total of 176,284 had left the factory gates, with many thousands more having been imported.

BMC Australia was also the most prolific manufacturer of the Mini Moke, whose story is told in full in *SECTION EIGHT*.

Innocenti

Innocenti or, to give it its full name, *Innocenti Societa Generale per l'Industria Metallurgica e Meccanica SpA*, began life under Ferdinand Innocenti in 1933. After the war, its main claim to fame was the manufacture of the Lambretta motor scooter. The Milan-based company branched out into car manufacture in 1960 when it undertook licensed production of the Austin A40.

The Innocenti Mini-Cooper 1300 Export was the ultimate Italian-built Mini. It had a 66bhp 1,275cc engine, capable of taking the Cooper to 95mph. Note the unique Innocenti winding windows and swivelling quarter-lights.

For many years thereafter, all its collaborations were with BMC: first it offered a special-bodied Austin-Healey Sprite, then took on manufacture of the Austin/Morris 1100. In October 1965, it took the momentous step of manufacturing the Mini, using mechanical and some body parts imported from Britain. Italy quickly became the largest export market for the Mini.

The Italian Mini was known as the Innocenti Mini-Minor 850 and was always slightly superior to the British Mini. Its specification in the year of launch included Hydrolastic suspension, opening rear quarter-windows, lever-pull door handles,

ribbed vinyl trim, rubber mats and a three-gauge oval dial. Its distinguishing features over a Longbridge Mini were oval Innocenti badges, a chrome grille with nine horizontal bars, a plinth under the bumper for the small Italian number-plate, extra little round indicators on the sides of the front wings, rear light clusters incorporating reversing lights, and white, not orange, lenses under the headlamps.

The Mini-Minor sold for 860,000 *lire*, which was quite expensive compared with its Italian competition like the Fiat 850. However, the Innocenti was certainly far more sophisticated than the

Details of the Innocenti Mini-Cooper 1300 Export. The dashboard was a veritable feast of gauges for Mini drivers used to making do with niggardly British-specification facias.

The new Innocenti Mini series launched in 1974 replaced the Issigonis-style shell with one penned by Bertone. Developed in close liaison with Longbridge, it could easily have replaced the Mini in Britain. This is a 998cc Mini 90.

The more powerful Mini 120 used the 1,275cc engine and was easily distinguished by its chrome bumpers. The mechanical elements of the Innocenti were identical to its predecessor.

at 5,800rpm and 48lb.ft (SAE) of torque at 3,000rpm. Thus its top speed was quoted as 84mph.

Also in 1968 came the Mini-Cooper Mk2. This had special wheels, different trim and a 9.5:1 compression 998cc engine with 60bhp (SAE) available. Innocenti quoted a top speed of 93mph for its home-built version of the Mini-Cooper.

Following the revised MkIII Minis in Britain, Innocenti revised its entire range in 1970 with the Mini-Minor Mk3, Mini t Mk3 and Mini-Cooper Mk3. They all gained the familiar concealed door

Fiat and became a very familiar sight on Italian roads.

Making its debut at the Turin Show in 1966, Innocenti next added the Mini estate model to its range, which it called the Mini t. Like its British cousin, it was offered in all-metal and wood-trimmed versions.

Innocenti offered its own Mini-Cooper from March 1966. This was again very similar to the UK-built Cooper, but added the usual Innocenti touches. It had the standard Mini-Cooper 998cc engine, offering identical performance to the standard Longbridge Cooper.

In 1968 came the Mini-Minor Mk2 with all the body improvements seen in the British-made MkII. It retained Innocenti's unique front indicator arrangement and different badging, but was in most other respects identical to the British Mini MkII. Yet while earlier versions of the Innocenti Mini had kept the mechanical side of things the same, the Mini-Minor Mk2 had an 848cc engine with a 9:1 compression ratio and an HS4 carburettor, giving it a higher 48bhp (SAE)

hinges, but the front windows, although they wound down, incorporating swivelling quarter-lights. All but the Mini t estate car also retained for some time the old Hydrolastic system abandoned by British Mini saloons in 1969.

The Cooper Mk3 had a quite different facia from all the other Mini models, which followed their British counterparts to a large degree. It came with a full-width facia containing no less than five faired-in dials, a speedo and rev-counter in the centre of the dash and three minor gauges sited, strangely, in front of the driver. There also appeared a new Mini-Matic, with the four-speed AP automatic gearbox and standard 998cc engine.

In May 1972, Innocenti was bought up by BL following the death of Ferdinand Innocenti. The Italian operation had been extremely profitable for BL: more Minis were sold in Italy than any other foreign country (an annual average of 55,000 was recorded during the early Seventies). So rather than let control move to an unsympathetic outsider, it took Innocenti over and renamed it Leyland Innocenti SpA. BL man

Geoffrey Robinson became the new Chairman.

At that time, the range was jigged about. The Mini-Minor became the Mini 1000, there was a new model called the 1001 (basically an upmarket 1000), the Mini-Matic, the Mini T1000 estate and a new Mini-Cooper 1300. All models now came with rubber-cone springing and had revised black grilles with a distinct shape of their own and a prominent horizontal chrome strip across them broken by a new 'Mini' motif and the appropriate badge for the model concerned. Leyland badges appeared on the bonnet and front wings. The 1001 could be identified by its unique hubcaps, wood-finish oval instrument binnacle and special badging. The 1001 also had a more powerful 9:1 compression 51bhp 998cc engine.

The Cooper 1300 was the equivalent of a Mini-Cooper 1275S in specification and offered a top speed of 95mph. It was allowed to continue in production after the British Cooper had died because Innocenti had not signed to the same royalty agreements. It had wider tyres and hence came with screw-on wheelarch spats.

The final true Innocenti Mini variant, the Mini-Cooper 1300 Export of March 1973, was a revised Cooper with new interior treatment, rod-type gearchange and dual-circuit brakes.

Innocenti Minis were always good sellers in Italy, where a monthly production rate of around 2,800 was typical, and a grand total of around 450,000 Minis of all varieties were made by Innocenti between 1965 and 1976. Although the Italian Mini and Mini-Cooper survived until the end of Leyland's involvement with Innocenti in 1975, with the final examples built up from old stock in 1976, they were all swept aside by

Innocenti's brand-new models: the Mini 90 and Mini 120.

Launched in 1974, the cars were externally all-new, with smart, angular steel bodywork by Bertone and a rear hatchback. Yet under the new Innocenti Mini, the old Mini platform remained, still retaining the same rubber-cone suspension, the same A-series engine/gearbox configuration, the same steering and brakes. The Mini 90 used the familiar 998cc engine, while the 120 had a detuned (65bhp) version of the 1,275cc engine which had previously been used in the Cooper 1300. There was a new exhaust and the radiator was resited in front of the engine.

If anything, the Innocenti was even better packaged than the Mini, with more space usable by the passengers as a percentage of the total volume of the car. The rear seats folded, greatly enhancing practicality, although the rear hatch had a very high loading lip.

Although the wheelbase was only marginally

A hatchback body was what the world wanted. Although having quite a high lip, the Innocenti was certainly made more practical by the addition of a rear hatch. Apart from rear headroom, packaging was a strong point.

The bizarre interior of the Innocenti Mini 120, with its square cut-out dials.

increased, the new Mini was 2.6in longer and 3.5in wider than the original Mini, but that was still significantly less than all other three-door hatchbacks (which were still a novelty in 1974). Weight was also significantly up to around 1,600lb (725kg); 12in wheels were standard.

The Mini 90 was fitted with a 9:1 compression 998cc engine with 49bhp on tap, giving it a claimed top speed of 87mph. The 120's twin-carburettor 1,275cc engine was engineered with a 9.75:1 compression ratio, enough for 65bhp at 5,600rpm and a top speed of 96mph. The driving experience was understandably very similar to the old Mini. The Mini 90 was slightly less well-equipped than the 120 and could be distinguished most easily by its matt black, rather than chrome, bumpers.

The Innocenti's interior was all-new. The dashboard was the most striking feature, with its peculiar square dials. The driving position was pure Mini, but the fitments and trim were far superior. Space was still fairly cramped – rear headroom was particularly poor – and there were some problems with body rigidity.

Autocar tested a Mini 120 in 1975 and concluded that, "as a replacement for the ubiquitous Mini, the Innocenti 90 and 120 models are a success", and questioned whether the cars might be sold in Britain. After all, the mechanical elements and many of the body pressings were actually made in Britain. BL did draw up plans for UK production at a rate of 5,000 cars per year, but somehow never had the courage to go ahead. The Innocenti Mini was much more expensive to make than the Mini and BL was stumbling from one financial crisis to the next throughout the Seventies. In retrospect, it is probably fortunate that BL never went ahead with large-scale manufacture of the Innocenti, although BL's range was seriously hampered by the lack of a three-door hatchback until the arrival of the Mini Metro of 1980. The Innocenti, although pretty, was not the timeless design which the Mini is and would have required expensive replacement within a few years.

BL's financial problems eventually forced it to sell its interest in Innocenti when Leyland Innocenti went into liquidation in summer 1975. Fending off interest from Fiat, De Tomaso took a controlling interest in April 1976 to create *Nuova Innocenti SpA*. Alessandro De Tomaso added his own Mini De Tomaso to the range, based on the Innocenti Mini 120. This had a 74bhp version of the 1,275cc A-series engine, powerful enough to accelerate the little car from 0–60mph in 12sec.

In all but name, the Innocenti severed its Mini connections when, in April 1982, it launched the new Mini 3 with three-cylinder powertrains from Daihatsu. By that time, Innocenti had made a creditable 220,000 of the new-shape Minis. Eventually, even the name changed, to Innocenti Small. In 1990, Fiat bought out De Tomaso and production of the Small finished in 1993. By 1994, Innocenti was merely a name under which Fiat sells the Brazilian-made Fiat Elba in Italy.

After Leyland cut its losses and pulled out of Italy, Alessandro de Tomaso bought Innocenti and immediately launched the Mini De Tomaso – a sharp and modern Italian equivalent of a Mini-Cooper.

AUTHI Mini

BMC's Madrid-based Spanish subsidiary was known as *Automoviles de Turismo Hispano Ingleses SA* (or AUTHI for short), where production of several BMC models took place, including the Morris 1100 and MG 1300, and a local version of the South African-designed Austin Apache, which was known as the Austin Victoria.

The first Mini built at AUTHI's Pamplona factory was the 1275C from October 1968. This was joined the following year by the more basic 1000E and 1000S models. The firm's name changed to Leyland Authi in 1969 following a majority buy-out by BL. The new regime also instituted production of 850 and 1275 GT Minis. In the Seventies, both the 850 and 1000 models were made in basic and 'Lujo' (later called de Luxe) versions. There was also a 1000LS model.

Mini-Coopers were made from October 1973. The Mini-Cooper 1300 produced by AUTHI was almost identical to the Innocenti Mini-Cooper 1300, down to much of its interior. It lasted until 1975 – almost as long as the Innocenti.

Production of all BMC cars ceased in 1976 as General Motors took over the plant, eventually turning it over to production of the Opel Corsa.

South African Minis

Leyland South Africa (Pty) Ltd made Minis throughout the Seventies. These mirrored closely the style of the Mini in Britain, but had a number of differences.

The base engine was the 1,098cc unit. This was fitted to both the De Luxe (standard Mini shell) and the Clubman. South Africa also had a unique Mini GTS model, which was basically a 1275

GT, but with a thick black body stripe and 'GTS' decals to identify it. All South African Minis had reflectors mounted on their front end.

One bizarre South African variant was a Mini with a Riley Elf-style rear end mated to a standard Mini saloon front.

The swansong Mini for South Africa was the 1275E of 1980, which was basically a Clubman shell with a 9.4:1 compression 1,275cc engine developing 56bhp at 5,000rpm. Unlike the British 1275 GT, it had 10in plain steel wheels (with 145/SD10 tyres) and drum brakes all round. Thick twin black coachlines down the body sides distinguished the model.

South American Minis: Chile

Of all the locally-produced versions of the Mini worldwide, the Chilean Mini was the strangest. In order to build a Mini in Chile, where there were no facilities for pressing metal and laws governing the amount of local labour required, it was necessary to develop a glassfibre lookalike bodyshell.

In appearance, it was quite different in detail from the metal Mini: there were no external flanges or roof gutters, for example, and there was a prominent ridge along the lower body sides. The Chilean plastic Mini was not made beyond the Seventies.

Venezuela

Rover decided to relaunch the Mini in the South American market for the Nineties with a second locally-produced Mini, again made from glass-

A South African-built Mini 1275E of 1980. This was the equivalent of a Mini 1275GT, but with wide 10in wheels and drum brakes.

South American Mini: this is the glassfibre-bodied Mini made in Chile during the late Sixties. Note the lack of any external seams – there was no welding! – and the thick wheelarch and sill line. *(BMIHT)*

fibre. This time, it collaborated with Facorca of Caracas, Venezuela. The first prototype was finished in April 1991. Like Chile, strict laws governing the proportion of locally-made content meant that a British-made steel bodyshell was impossible, so a locally-built plastic shell was developed instead.

On to mechanical components, including the 998cc Powerpack supplied from Longbridge, Facorca added its own glassfibre replica of a Mini bodyshell. The result was known as the MiniCord, and was earmarked to sell all over South and Central America and the Caribbean.

Mini Special Editions abroad

As well as the familiar special editions Mini produced for the UK market, numerous limited editions were developed especially for certain countries. Some were merely changes of name (eg Mini Masters instead of Advantage in Germany); others were unique to a particular market.

For instance, there was a unique 20th anniversary edition in New Zealand. In Germany, the

This late-Seventies Dutch 'Ebony' edition was based on the Mini 1000. It was painted black with contrasting stripes and had a tartan interior trim.

Made in France in the late Seventies, the Mini S was based on the Mini 1000 GL. Painted in blue with red stripes, it had blue velour seats, wheeltrims, extra indicators on the front wings and a leather steering wheel.

Based on the Mini 1100 Special, this 1979 French 'Printemps' had a wooden dash and gear knob, tartan upholstery, special stripes, tinted glass and a leather steering wheel.

importers sold the Thirty and Flame Red editions with locally-made styling kits and wood trim. Several continental markets also modified Belgian-built Minis to create unique editions in the Seventies.

France has received many unique editions with names like Twinings, After Eight and Woodbury; the 35th anniversary Mini was sold in Italy with a much higher specification under the name 35° Classic. The bewildering array of foreign special editions is almost impossible to document; suffice to say that the family will continue to grow.

This 1989 German 'Thirty' edition was similar to the British-market Mini Thirty, but with body styling kit and wooden dashboard.

Similar to the British-market Mini Flame Red, this 1990 German 'Flame Red' also came with a choice of LAMM or Sabwa body styling kits, and wood interior cappings.

The car above is a 1977 Mini LE marketed by the New Zealand Motor Corporation. Special features on this limited edition model included wheeltrims, side stripes, matt black grille, vinyl roof, carpeted boot, leather gear knob and brushed nylon seats and facia. A Clubman version was also sold.

The 1991 'Twinings' edition, made in France, was based on the 998cc Mini Mayfair. Painted black with gold coachlines, it had 'Twinings' decals on the flanks and steering wheel, and a removable remote-control stereo.

Based on the 998cc Mini Sprite, the 1992 French 'After Eight' special edition was painted British Racing Green with gold coachlines, and came with 'After Eight' motifs on the body and steering wheel and had velour upholstery.

Based on the 1,275cc Mini Sprite, this 1992 French 'Woodbury' edition was black with gold coachlines, had wood facia and door cappings, and beige leather upholstery.

APPENDIX A

Mini Clubs

As the Mini has been elevated to a position as an enthusiast's car – and a genuine classic – so the need has arisen for owners' clubs devoted to the Mini and its derivatives. During the Eighties, the club scene literally exploded into life, and spurred on by gigantic anniversary celebrations and the support offered by membership, their popularity has risen to astounding heights.

The following is a selection of owners' clubs catering for the Mini, with relevant contact information applicable at the time this book went to press. A complete list of all the local, international and specialist interest clubs would take several pages. Details of the smaller clubs and registers can usually be obtained from other enthusiasts in one of the bigger clubs, or from the International Mini Club Register (details below).

Mini Owners' Club

Formed in 1979 by Chris Cheal, the Mini Owners' Club remains the largest Mini club in the world, around 12,500 members having joined since inception and, at the time of writing, with 6,500 on the books. MOC has official approval from the Rover Group. There are numerous individual registers within the club for models like the 1275 GT, Innocenti and MkI and it has many regional groups who hold regular meetings. A quarterly magazine, club regalia, guidebook to specialists, insurance scheme and a spares service are all offered to members.

Contact: 15 Birchwood Road, LICHFIELD, Staffs WS14 9UN. Tel: 0543 257956.

Mini-Cooper Club

Also formed in 1979, the Mini-Cooper Club caters for all Minis, and especially Coopers (of all types). Membership is around 500. Events include treasure hunts and summer camps and there are registers for each Cooper model. A magazine is published four to six times a year, with 'For Sale' and 'Wanted' columns, technical advice, insurance schemes and regalia.

Contact: 38 Arbour House, Arbour Square, LONDON E1 0PP. Tel: 071-790 7060.

Mini-Cooper Register

Formed in 1986, the Mini-Cooper Register is a club for all Minis, although it obviously specializes in the Mini-Cooper. With just under 2,000 members, it is a national club with many local regional groups. There are separate registers for each of the Mini-Cooper types, including foreign-built Coopers and Rover Coopers. The MCR holds a National Mini-Cooper Day at Beaulieu every June, plus other events including test days. There is a monthly magazine with details of insurance schemes, technical tips, cars and parts for sale and so on.

Contact: Philip Splett. Tel: 0702 216062. Fax: 0702 217501.

Riley Motor Club

The RMC is the second oldest car club in the world, having been founded in 1925. It has about 1,500 members, including a large following for Elfs. The club offers a spares service, technical advice, a library service, insurance valuations, local meetings and national rallies, plus a magazine once every two months.

Contact: Treelands, 127 Penn Road, WOLVERHAMPTON WV3 0DU.

Wolseley Register

Although it is a club for all types of Wolseley, the Register does cater for Hornets. Founded in 1964, it has 1,100 members, a large number of whom are Hornet owners. There are local groups and an annual National Rally.

Contact: 6 Ezard St, Newtown, STOCKTON-ON-TEES, Cleveland TS19 0BZ.

Mini Moke Club

The Moke Club has been going since 1983 and now has 250 members. All Mokes and Moke enthusiasts are catered for, including Australian and Portuguese Mokes. Registers exist. It holds one large annual event plus a yearly visit to Portmeirion – where *The Prisoner* TV series was filmed – plus regional groups organizing local events. Regalia section (including Mini Moke sticks of rock!), and support for parts suppliers and some remanufacture of parts.

Contact: Highgate, Leys Lane, MERIDEN CV7 7LQ. Tel: 0676 22372.

Mini Special Register

Set up in 1990 and run by Adrian Boyns, MSR caters for the following special edition Minis: 1100 Special, 25, 30, 35, Belgian Special and New Zealand Anniversary. There are currently 120 members. Spares and regalia are available.

Contact: 47 Hest View, ULVERSTON, Cumbria LA12 9PH. Tel: 0229 584132.

International Mini Club Register

Started by David Vizard in 1980, the Register lists every known Mini club worldwide: that's over 300 from some 34 countries. The IMCR promotes international contact and co-operation between clubs and their members.

Contact: Martin Bell, 151 Waverley Road, Stoneleigh, EPSOM, Surrey KT17 2LN.

APPENDIX B

Mini production worldwide by year

	Year-by-year	Cumulative total
1959	19,749	19,749
1960	116,677	136,426
1961	157,059	293,485
1962	216,087	509,572
1963	236,713	746,285
1964	244,359	990,644
1965	221,974	1,212,618
1966	213,694	1,426,312
1967	237,227	1,663,539
1968	246,066	1,909,605
1969	254,957	2,164,562
1970	278,950	2,443,512
1971	318,475	2,761,987
1972	306,937	3,068,924
1973	295,186	3,364,110
1974	255,336	3,619,446
1975	200,293	3,819,739
1976	203,575	4,023,314
1977	214,134	4,237,448
1978	196,799	4,434,247
1979	165,502	4,599,749
1980	150,067	4,749,816
1981	69,986	4,819,802
1982	56,297	4,876,099
1983	49,956	4,926,055
1984	35,038	4,961,093
1985	34,974	4,996,067
1986	33,720	5,029,787
1987	37,210	5,066,997
1988	36,574	5,103,571
1989	40,998	5,144,569
1990	46,045	5,190,614
1991	35,007	5,225,621
1992	26,197	5,251,818
1993	20,468	5,272,286
1994 (Jan–Apr)	8,579	5,280,865

These figures represent the total of all Minis and official Mini derivatives made worldwide. Inevitably, they cannot be totally reliable as there are many grey areas in the counting procedures. In particular, there are question marks over the inclusion of accurate Moke figures, and Seneffe production records appear to be incomplete.

Mini production breakdown by model

These figures are approximations rather than definitives because the production records are not always clear as to the precise model manufactured.

Mini MkI

Austin Se7en/Mini saloon	435,000
Morris Mini-Minor saloon	510,000
Austin Countryman	85,500
Morris Traveller	75,500
Total	**1,106,000**

Mini MkII

Austin Mini saloon	154,000
Morris Mini saloon	206,000
Austin Countryman	22,500
Morris Traveller	23,500
Total	**406,000**

Mini-Cooper MkI

Austin Mini-Cooper 997cc	12,395
Morris Mini-Cooper 997cc	12,465
Austin Mini-Cooper 998cc	17,737
Morris Mini-Cooper 998cc	21,627
Total	**64,224**

Mini-Cooper MkII

Austin Mini-Cooper	9,168
Morris Mini-Cooper	7,228
Total	**16,396**

Mini-Cooper 'S' MkI

Austin Mini-Cooper 'S' 1,071cc	2,135
Morris Mini-Cooper 'S' 1,071cc	1,896
Austin Mini-Cooper 'S' 970cc	481
Morris Mini-Cooper 'S' 970cc	482
Austin Mini-Cooper 'S' 1,275cc	6,489
Morris Mini-Cooper 'S' 1,275cc	7,824
Total	**19,307**

Mini-Cooper 'S' MkII

Austin Mini-Cooper 'S'	2,687
Morris Mini-Cooper 'S'	3,642
Total	**6,329**

Mini-Cooper 'S' MkIII

Total	**19,511**

Mini MkIII

Mini 850	407,670
Mini 1000/City/Mayfair	1,439,819
Mini Clubman saloon	275,583
Mini Clubman estate (incl HL)	197,606
Mini 1275 GT	110,673
Mini 1100	78,853
Mini 1300 (export only)	21,360
Mini Sprite/Mayfair (to April 1994)	35,423
Mini-Cooper commemorative	1,650
Mini-Cooper carburettor	19,899
Mini-Cooper 1.3i (to April 1994)	21,034
Mini Cabriolet (LAMM)	75
Mini Cabriolet (Rover) (to April 1994)	414
Total (to April 1994)	**2,610,059**

Mini Van

Austin Minivan	174,500
Morris Minivan	169,249
Mini Van 850	94,899
Mini Van 1000	82,356
Total	**521,494**

Mini Pick-up

Austin Mini Pick-up	18,000
Morris Mini Pick-up	12,652
Mini Pick-up 850	12,130
Mini Pick-up 1000	15,397
Total	**58,179**

Mini Moke

Austin Mini Moke	5,422
Morris Mini Moke	9,096
Total	**14,518**
Australian Moke	26,142
Portuguese Moke (to end 1992)	9,277

Riley Elf

Elf MkI	3,522
Elf MkII	17,816
Elf MkIII	9,574
Total	30,912

Wolseley Hornet

Hornet MkI	3,166
Hornet MkII	16,785
Hornet MkIII	8,504
Total	28,455

Sales in the UK by year

1959	7,800
1960	63,900
1961	95,000
1962	116,000
1963	134,346
1964	123,429
1965	103,147
1966	91,697
1967	82,436
1968	86,185
1969	68,061
1970	80,562
1971	102,006
1972	96,185
1973	96,383
1974	89,686
1975	84,688
1976	81,107
1977	60,337
1978	72,617
1979	82,938
1980	61,129
1981	28,772
1982	25,503
1983	27,739
1984	23,329
1985	18,559
1986	16,154
1987	15,873
1988	14,108
1989	12,852
1990	10,067
1991	8,531
1992	6,809
1993	6,326

Best Mini markets

1980

1	UK	61,129
2	France	14,290
3	Italy	5,343
4	Ireland	2,916
5	Netherlands	2,820
6	Belgium	2,468
7	Germany	2,291
8	Portugal	2,110

(NB Japan = 201)

1990

1	Japan	12,087
2	UK	10,067
3	France	8,977
4	Germany	4,790
5	Italy	2,680
6	Netherlands	1,401
7	Belgium	630
8	Taiwan	557
9	Portugal	131
10	Ireland	106

1993

1	Japan	8,681
2	UK	6,326
3	France	3,578
4	Germany	2,970
5	Italy	2,007
6	Netherlands	598
7	Belgium	406
8	Spain	177

The Mini LS of 1977 was a swansong luxury Aussie Mini. Standard features included magnesium wheels, foglamps, vinyl roof, cloth sports seats, rev-counter and metallic paint. Both 998cc and 1,275cc versions became available.